THE ADDICTION HANDBOOK BY JESUS

Identifying the Biblical Root of Addiction

Chaplain Tim Klink

November 2017

Prison Discipleship Ministry
P.O. Box 645   Massillon, OH 44648

THE ADDICTION HANDBOOK BY JESUS

Copyright © 2017 Timothy C. Klink

All scripture quotations are from the King James Version 1611, also known as the Authorized Version.

Published by Prison Discipleship Ministry, P.O. Box 645, Massillon, OH 44648.

Printed in the United States of America

THE ADDICTION HANDBOOK BY JESUS

Contents

The Addiction Handbook by Jesus

Introduction

The title of this document, "The Addiction Handbook by Jesus" was chosen because everything contained within has its foundation in the words written in Mark 5:2 defining the root of anything that controls a person, other than the Holy Spirit of God, as an "unclean spirit." With that definition established and confirmed by scripture, we see how Jesus proceeds to simply rid the one controlled of what it is that is controlling him, as well as keep the unclean spirit from controlling in the future. It is not the purpose of this document to discredit addiction recovery programs since important information may be gained from them concerning life skills needed to live a clean and productive life after addiction. The purpose of this is to point out the need to identify and eliminate the source of all addiction before lifestyle can be successfully altered.

Chaplain Tim Klink

Section 1   Chapter 1   Addiction Defined

What qualifies as an "addiction" and who can be considered as an "addict"? The day we live in seems to be filled with stories of people who are addicted to one thing or another. The most obvious, and what dominates the media, is the drug addiction problem. When the word "addiction" or "addict" is mentioned most people immediately think of illegal drug use.

But the term "addiction" or "addict" is much broader than just drugs or alcohol as we will see. It is not the purpose of this document to explore everything a person can be addicted to; but rather to identify the source or root of the addictive element from the Word of God, the Bible, as well as explore how it demonstrates its release. To get the concept of the term "addict" let's look at how the word is defined in the Webster Dictionary of American English (1828).

"**Addict** - *To apply one's self habitually; to devote time and attention by customary or constant practice; sometimes in a good sense.*

They have addicted themselves [note: made themselves servants to] to the ministry of the saints. 1 Corinthians 16:15.

More usually, in a bad sense, to follow customarily, or devote, by habitually practicing that which is ill; as, a man is addicted to excess in any kind of action or indulgence."

If we were to condense that definition down to one statement I believe it would be this: Addiction is anything that controls you physically, mentally, or spiritually. This is a neutral statement of fact and does not carry with it either good or bad presumptions. For instance, when the Spirit of God is controlling a person it is good, but when the spirit of Satan is controlling a person it is sin. (A simple definition of sin is breaking God's Law). Again, it is not within the purpose of this document to explore the depths of the doctrine of sin, but to merely make the statement that anything that controls a person's life other than God's Holy Spirit is sin. That statement

4

can be reinforced throughout the Bible (Romans 3:23, Ezekiel 18:4, Genesis 2:17, etc.)

Addiction can be a good thing when it is directed towards the things of God. The verse sited within the definition above is a perfect example.

1 Corinthians 16:15 *I beseech you, brethren, (ye know the house of Stephanas, that it is the firstfruits of Achaia, and that they* **have addicted themselves to the ministry of the saints,**) (emphasis mine)

The household of Stephanas, one of the believers in the early church, was so occupied with helping other believers, including the apostle Paul, that he said they had *"addicted themselves to the ministry."* What was controlling their thoughts, their motives, as well as their actions was serving others through the gospel. This meant not only preaching and teaching concerning the Lord Jesus Christ, but helping as they were able to meet the physical, emotional, and spiritual needs of those around them, especially those in the church. From this we can see how something good can be so controlling that it can be said to be an addiction. What makes the difference in the direction an addiction takes in a person's life is the object of that addiction. With these believers the central object and focus was on Jesus Christ.

When the object changes to self the entire outcome of the addiction changes. When greed, pleasure, pride, and any number of selfish motives are catered to and allowed to become a controlling force in a person's life the outcome is sin. The most notable of these controlling forces are drugs, alcohol, and sex. Things such as destructive lifestyles are just as sinful. These can include overeating or eating a poor diet, frequenting places which are not God honoring, an explosive temper, or allowing ungodly things to enter your mind through television or the internet, etc. Keep the definition of "addict" in mind as you consider what may be controlling your life.

As you set forth to see the things Jesus would have you see concerning addiction there is one thing that must be established and agreed upon before we can proceed which is

5

the fact that God cannot lie! In order for what you are about to read and consider in this document to be effective in your life you must have that fact firmly planted in your heart and mind. God's Word is Truth and it will never change.

Malachi 3:6 *For I am the LORD, I change not....*

With that stated let's begin the journey of seeing what Jesus Christ, the very Son of God has to say about addiction.

Chapter 2   Marks of an Addict; the Source, and Deliverance in Jesus

Mark 5:1-20

Mark 5:1-2 *And they came over unto the other side of the sea, into the country of the Gadarenes. (2) And when he [Jesus] was come out of the ship, immediately there met him out of the tombs a man with an unclean spirit,*

The first thing that stands out in this portion of scripture is the word "immediately." In Mark 4:35-41 we see the account of the voyage Jesus and the disciples took across the Sea of Galilee, and how they encountered a "great storm" which God used to guide them to the exact piece of ground where this man was to meet them. Not only were they geographically in the correct place, but they arrived at the exact moment in time when the man would be there. We will deal with this portion of scripture in chapter seven, "Why A Storm?"

Here, however, it is noteworthy to see the amazing power Jesus Christ has in directing lives, nature, circumstances, and all things to accomplish God's will. We often tend to criticize things that God is controlling because we do not completely understand His ultimate purpose and will for our lives. As a jail chaplain I deal with men and women who are of the opinion that they are incarcerated because God is somehow punishing them for what they did and that He hates them. It is such a privilege to show them that just the opposite is true and that their incarceration is all a part of God's plan to bring them into a marvellous relationship with Him. When that is realized there is hope.

Jesus used the storm upon the sea to direct that ship to exactly where the need was. He will also direct in your life if you will allow Him to do so. Sometimes it may take a "storm" and sometimes it may take a "great storm" to get you onto the course and path He has for you. The severity of the "storm" is dependent upon your stubbornness to listen to and obey God's Word as He attempts to guide you.

All addictions begin with a first choice. It is at that moment that a decision is made to indulge in something that you know is wrong in God's sight, but you decide to do it anyway. Man's desire for pleasure, greed, revenge, etc. is a powerful force and the process of reason becomes clouded. For instance, a young person who picks up their first cigarette has seen the pictures and heard the accounts of smokers who are suffering greatly with lung cancer and other diseases caused by the addiction, but they still take that first puff. The second puff becomes "easier" on the conscience until they are totally hooked and have ignored all of the warnings God has given them. The "storm" for that person will be greater than the "storm" for the person that walks away from the temptation early in obedience to God's warnings and direction.

Mark 5:2 *And when he was come out of the ship, immediately there met him out of the tombs a man with an unclean spirit,*

Jesus identified the root of the problem immediately - an "unclean spirit." The first reaction a person in this day and age may have to the mention of an "unclean spirit" is a mental picture of something spooky, or of Casper from their childhood. The spooky, spirit aspect is a product of Hollywood and the entertainment industry. Today, everyone knows that this is just entertainment and adds a "scare factor" to life, so the thought of spirits, let alone unclean spirits, is just something that was taken seriously "back in the day," but certainly not today. Probably the greatest deception Satan has ever pulled off, and continues to be successful with, is to get human beings to believe he does not exist. Reason would have it, if Satan does not actually exist then neither does his hordes of demons. Why would anyone fear something that does not exist? The mindset becomes like the day you finally realized that monsters do not live under the bed.

Most people do not know exactly what they believe when it comes to the spirit world since there has been so much falseness proclaimed over the years. The only source of truth is God and His Word. Consider what Jesus had to say about the spirit world:

8

John 4:24 *God is a Spirit: and they that worship him must worship him in spirit and in truth.*

Jesus was on His way from Judea to Cana and stopped to rest. He sat on the edge of a well and asked a lady who had come to draw water for herself to draw Him some water also. As they talked they spoke about worship and the woman indicated that *"our fathers worshipped in this mountain, and ye say, that in Jerusalem is the place where men ought to worship"* (John 4:20). Jesus then told her the above statement that *"God is a Spirit."* In John 10:30 Jesus states, *"I and my Father are one."* While Jesus was upon this earth He was all human and all God (spirit).

Next, consider the angels. In Psalm 104 verse 4 David proclaimed as he wrote of the marvellous attributes of God, *"Who maketh his angels spirits; his ministers a flaming fire."* Angels do not have human bodies and are totally spirit. Lucifer was one of those created angels who was given great beauty and a position of high power in the government of God (Isaiah 14). His rebellion against God (Isaiah 14:13-14) made him the enemy of God who attacks those whom God loves, namely human beings. Lucifer's name was changed to Satan and he remains a spirit being along with all of the angel host that followed him in his rebellion against God. These are Satan's demons.

Without getting aside from our main topic, what I want you to realize is that there is a very real spiritual world in existence and it was created by God Himself for His purpose and glory. Reason would show us that God as well as Satan, being spirit, would communicate with man on a spiritual level and not with a physical, audible voice as we communicate among ourselves. Man, having been created (Genesis 2:7) with a body (physical) and soul (spirit), is able to communicate with God as well as Satan. This is accomplished through the thoughts of man.

Have you ever had the urge to read your Bible or to attend a church service or to pray? That is the work of God's Holy Spirit communicating with you through your thoughts and attempting to guide you in the direction God would have you go. That could be considered a "clean spirit." On the other side, have you ever had the urge to do something you knew was wrong such as tell a lie or cheat in a situation you found yourself in? Have you ever had the urge to partake in some inappropriate action or speech? That is the "unclean spirit" of Satan and his demons trying to get you to go against the leadership of God. All of this communication is accomplished within your thoughts. I am certainly not claiming there are no such things as actual demons because there are. What I am attempting to get you to realize is that the way they communicate their wicked desires to you is through your thoughts. These are called temptations.

Deception is the main method Satan uses to get you to consider and act upon his temptations. His subtilty (Genesis 3:1) is greater than anything man can resist apart from the power of God. One of his sly thoughts is for you to just "follow your heart," or "if it feels good do it," and the classic "everyone else is doing it." That is the "voice" of an unclean spirit. It is nothing spooky or weird as the media has projected, but the simple entertaining of a thought from an unclean spirit to do something against God. Have you ever had an evil or wicked thought? Have you ever wanted to take revenge on someone that wronged you? Have you ever been tempted to tell a lie? That is the communication from an unclean spirit!

Temptation in itself is not a sin. When you allow temptation to remain in your mind and consider it as something you like to think about, it then becomes sin. Sexual and pornographic thoughts are a perfect example. As a chaplain I have worked with many people who during their incarceration admit that the thing that is in their thoughts the most is getting out and "getting high." Those thoughts, if allowed to remain will eventually result in actions that are against God's direction. Someone once said, you cannot stop someone from ringing your doorbell; but you can stop them from coming into your house for a cup of coffee. In other words when you allow the tempting thought from the unclean spirit to remain it will usually result in actions that align themselves with the temptation. If you are tempted to steal, and allow that temptation to remain in your mind, the odds are very favorable that you will steal. We will look deeper into resisting temptation in chapter seven.

As the unclean spirit continues to put thoughts which are against God's will into a person's mind, and these thoughts are allowed to remain, the person will yield a portion of control to them. The more these thoughts are entertained the more control is given to them until the unclean spirit has the majority of control over the thoughts and actions of that person. This is the state of mind the man in verse 2 is in. The unclean spirit has taken almost total control over him.

Mark 5:3-4 *Who had his dwelling among the tombs; and no man could bind him, no, not with chains: (4) Because that he had been often bound with fetters and chains, and the chains had been plucked asunder by him, and the fetters broken in pieces: neither could any man tame him.*

Living among the tombs of the dead is not a normal thing. This man was so under the control of the unclean spirit that he had been evicted from dwelling among others and only found acceptance among those who did not object to his radical behavior – the dead. Historically the tombs in the hills around Gadara were where thieves and others outside of the law stayed as well as those who were social outcasts. Living among the tombs is not socially acceptable and is a culture all its own with a mindset of lawlessness and rebellion against authority.

The control, or addiction, an unclean spirit can exert upon a person will often lead to a fascination with death and the things of the bizarre. What else would one expect from Satan, the one who is the originator of the unclean spirit, and the father of all lies and evil? Most addictions will ultimately result in either physical or spiritual death, and often both. So, the first indication that the man in Mark 5 is an addict is his fascination with and closeness to the realm of the dead.

Next, we read that "*no man could bind him, no, not with chains.*" The men of that area were concerned about the behavior of this man and possibly feared his actions would harm them in some way. Their assumptions were well founded since anyone who is under the control of an unclean spirit in their life is capable of some very irrational behavior. Binding this man with chains was the only way they knew to subdue him and keep him from further harming himself as well as others. The same procedure is used today especially when man's law is broken. Incarceration is used to keep the addict under a certain amount of control and literal chains may be needed to keep him from harming himself or others, as well as helping to prevent escape.

Another form of "chains" that are used to bind or control one who is addicted to something are the recovery programs that are so popular in this day. Recovery programs attempt to teach different behavioral patterns so the addict can make proper choices in his life. There are certain "steps" that are to be learned and adopted in most programs and from a behavioral standpoint they are all good. However, the rate of return to the addiction over a period of time is high. Why is this? The answer lies in the free will God created within each of us. The chains and fetters (leg chains) were able to be *"plucked asunder by him"* and broken in pieces.

The key words are *"by him."* He had the strength as well as the determination to reject those chains and fetters just as a person has the God-given free will to reject the teaching of the programs placed upon him. The teachings and methods instilled through a program may be effective for a time but eventually most people will turn from them and return to their addiction. The source of the problem has not been dealt with. An example would be how a crew of firemen extinguishes a fire. They don't just pour a bunch of water on it and leave. They stay and make sure the source of any potential reignition is eliminated. If the source of an addiction is not dealt with it will reignite.

"...neither could any man tame him." What those who tried to tame him did not consider was the source, the unclean spirit. In their attempts to subdue or change this man they never once attempted to identify the source let alone deal with it. Directing an unclean spirit is not something that is within

the power or ability of human beings. Since the source was not dealt with the addictive behavior continued. Today man attempts to "tame" the one addicted through teachings and programs that are full of very good information, but in the end most addicts go away "untamed."

Mark 5:5 *And always, night and day, he was in the mountains, and in the tombs, crying, and cutting himself with stones.*

The control an addiction can have over a person is relentless. The one addicted to drugs is always looking for the next hit. The one addicted to alcohol is always looking for the next drink. The one addicted to sexual things is always looking for that which he can look at and lust after. Even the subtler addictions such as an uncontrolled, explosive temper, eating addictions, tobacco addiction, etc., keep their victim on constant alert for the next opportunity to indulge. "*Day and night*" there is no end to the ever growing but never satisfied draw of an addiction. This man was "*in the mountains,*" the highs of addiction; "*and in the tombs,*" the ever-deepening lows of depression before the next indulgence. He was "*crying*" in anguish looking for relief with no one able to help. One can almost imagine the sounds of wailing and utter despair coming through the night air as this poor, helpless man suffered under the relentless attack of the unclean spirit driving him even further into his addiction.

He was "*cutting himself with stones*" in a display of the low to almost non-existent self-esteem he had sunk to. His reasoning may have been seeking release even to the point of death from such a horrible task master as the unclean spirit had become. His cutting may have been a demonstration of the power it held over him. In any case he was doing damage to his own body which displays the driving force of destruction an unclean spirit holds over a person through the means of an addiction. The ultimate motive for an unclean spirit is to bring hurt to God by hurting the ones He loves.

(Mark 5:6) *But when he saw Jesus afar off, he ran and worshipped him,*

The entire reason why Jesus instructed the disciples to take Him *"unto the other side"* (Mark 4:35) was because this one man whom God loved dearly was in need of a Saviour/Deliverer. What was so special about this man to attract such personal attention from the very Son of God? Absolutely nothing! God's love through His Son Jesus was not dependent upon any good thing that he had done. One look at this man and it would stretch the imagination to see *any* "good thing" in him from man's perspective. When the man stood on the shore watching Jesus get out of the ship he was the same man who was totally controlled by the unclean spirit and his addiction was still intact. He didn't reason within himself that he needed to clean himself up before running to Jesus. He didn't need anyone else that was "better" than he was to accompany him. He didn't need to enter a structured program for a period of time and learn many new things about human behavior before his run to Jesus. He simply saw Jesus as the One who could help him and he took off running.

That must have been a very wonderful sight to Jesus to see this man running to Him since Jesus knew exactly why he was coming. Consider the scene from the perspective of the disciples. What they saw was a madman running at full steam towards their beloved Jesus. What was he going to do? Was he intending to bring harm to Jesus and them as well? That must have been a sight to see this man with scars from the cutting, badly in need of a haircut, shave, a bath, and clothing running towards them while Jesus stood firm with a smile on His face and in His heart welcoming him. What a graphic demonstration between the love Jesus has for those who are under the control of an unclean spirit and those who simply are watching from the sidelines. While others may be sympathetic and have all good intentions to help, only Jesus can deliver a person from the power and presence of an unclean spirit. Only Jesus can go to the source of the addiction and command the unclean spirit to *"come out of the man"* (verse 8).

When the man reached Jesus, he fell down at Jesus feet and *"worshipped Him."* This is a man that may or may not have had a previous knowledge of "religious" things. None of that mattered. The only thing that was needed was that he opened his heart to Jesus and allowed Jesus to do what only He can do. That is to love him, forgive him, and cleanse him from the unclean spirit that has him enslaved. He had been bound with the "*chains and fetters*" of men in their attempts to tame him; but this was the exact opposite of what Jesus did, which was to deliver him.

Taming is merely bringing a change of actions within the same attitudes and behavior as before. For instance, when it is said that a lion is tamed by a lion tamer, it means that the natural behavior of the lion has been changed to comply with the person's demands who is doing the taming. However, it is still a lion and it is still very capable of reverting back to its natural ways which are still all intact. When Jesus deals with a person they are not what they used to be, but are completely different. The old ways are gone. The old desires are gone. (2 Corinthians 5:17) *Therefore if any man be in Christ, he is a new creature: old things are passed away; behold, all things are become new.* We see this demonstrated in verse 15.

(Mark 5:15) *And they come to Jesus, and see him that was possessed with the devil, and had the legion, sitting, and clothed, and in his right mind: and they were afraid.*

This was the same human being they saw before but he was now a new creature. Jesus does not remodel the old heart, He replaces it with a completely new one. The man's appearance was different because he had a completely new set of values and goals. He wanted to serve Jesus instead of being under captivity to the unclean spirit. Where he was once running throughout the mountains and the tombs, we now see him "*sitting*" in the presence of Jesus and "*clothed*" with proper attire. More importantly, we see him clothed with the love of God wrapped around and through him. Where once he was "*crying*" for deliverance he now has peace. Where once he was "*cutting himself with stones*" he is now in his right mind.

What made the great difference in this man? What turned the bondage he suffered under for such a long time into peace as well as a purpose? It was not those who tried to help, and it certainly was not the chains and fetters. The only One that could possibly deliver him completely was Jesus. After first seeing Jesus "*afar off*" he realized there was something he needed and that the answer to his bondage was standing in his sight. Many times, we see Jesus afar off and wonder if He is truly the answer to our bondage. There is a decision that needs to be made at that moment and it is not a decision that will come without opposition from the enemy, the unclean spirit. Thoughts will enter our mind that try to give reasons why we should not trust Jesus with this great task. The unclean spirit will do everything it can to get you to turn from Jesus and leave things as they are. "Things will work out, just give it some time. You can slow down or you can change this or that about your addiction and it will be good. You don't need Jesus and all of that religious stuff," is what will flash into your mind in an instant.

The man in these verses was "*always, night and day, ... in the mountains, and in the tombs, crying, and cutting himself with stones.*" He greatly desired relief from his unclean spirit, but found none within himself or within others. He had to come to the point in his life where he realized that what he was doing to himself as well as others was not working out too well and that he needed a true Deliverer. He made the decision, the choice, to run to Jesus and to "*worship him.*" The term "worship" has many aspects, but in this case the man simply opened his heart to Jesus. He didn't sing praises to Him, he didn't listen to Him preach a sermon, he didn't take up an offering and give it to Jesus, he simply fell at Jesus' feet and humbly submitted himself to Him.

As you think about whatever may be controlling you and you consider this One called Jesus, the only thing that stands in the way of complete deliverance is you and your unwillingness to completely open your heart to Jesus. He knows every aspect of your life even before you go to Him. By coming to Jesus, the man was telling himself, telling the unclean spirit, and telling anyone else involved in his life that he cannot deal with his current situation and admitting whole-heartedly that Jesus is the only One who can. It is at that point that all attempts to change are given up and given to Jesus. Whatever controls you other than God's Holy Spirit is sin, and that must be the heart attitude you take before Jesus.

The penalty for your sin has been paid at a great cost to Jesus Christ on the cross. The extreme torture and agony He endured for hours at the hands of those who beat Him and crucified Him was all directed to pay for your sin personally, as well as the sin of all who have ever lived. Jesus has already paid the price for your freedom from the unclean spirit as well as for the payment of your sin. What will you do with Jesus? Will you trust Him and the work He accomplished for you or will you continue to listen to the unclean spirit that has got you to where you are today? You have been created with a free will by the same God that gave His only begotten Son Jesus for you; and you do have a choice.

(Mark 5:18) *And when he was come into the ship, he that had been possessed with the devil prayed him that he might be with him.*

When the decision was made to submit himself to Jesus he wanted to be with the One who had done such a great work in him. It is a natural thing to desire to be with those we love. The deeper that love the more we want to be in their presence and in their life. I love my children and grandchildren and would do anything for them, but the one I want to spend all of my time with is my wife of fifty years. As much as I want to be totally involved in her life and love, I want to spend all of my thoughts and actions in the love of Jesus which will flow out to others. This man did not want to just say thank you to Jesus and then return to the tombs and the old way of life. He was a "new creature" in Christ and those old things were not a part of anything he desired any more. Had he gone back to the tombs and to the old ways, even for only a "visit," the door of opportunity would have opened just enough for the unclean spirit to start all over in him.

While it is true that a genuine believer cannot be *possessed* by an unclean spirit, they sure can be *controlled* by them when allowed. The man didn't want to take any chances and wanted to make a complete break from the old paths. He didn't desire to return to the tombs. He didn't desire to cut himself anymore. He didn't want to be associated in any way with things of the past that controlled him; he wanted to simply dwell in the presence of the One who did such a marvellous work in his life.

(Mark 5:19) *Howbeit Jesus suffered him not, but saith unto him, Go home to thy friends, and tell them how great things the Lord hath done for thee, and hath had compassion on thee.*

Jesus had a different plan for his life. He had a plan that would bring much honor and glory to God while still remaining in the loving presence of Jesus in his heart and mind. Jesus said, "*Go home to thy friends.*" Not back to those who lived in the tombs. Not to the ones that he had run with while under the control of the unclean spirit. Those were not "friends" but tools of the enemy that sought to destroy him. The "friends" were those in his family and those who he knew prior to the addiction. The friends were those who would listen to what he had to tell. His message was not focused on himself and what all he had been through, but on the One who had delivered him despite his terrible condition. He was to proclaim the compassion that the Lord had shown to him and in doing so others would believe also.

When Jesus delivers a person from the control of an unclean spirit He has a purpose for that person which is to glorify God. It may be as simple as just telling others that it was Jesus who did it all. It may be something as great as preaching the gospel to multitudes of people. Either way glory is given to God for His marvellous love and compassion on those who have done nothing but sin against Him. The saddest and rudest thing a person can do when someone gives them a gift is not to give thanks back to them for it. The gift of salvation and deliverance from the unclean spirits that control us is the greatest gift of all time, and yet there are many who walk away having received that gift and never return thanks to God by serving Him.

(Mark 5:20) *And he departed, and began to publish in Decapolis how great things Jesus had done for him: and all men did marvel.*

This man did not walk away and forget his assignment, but went over and above in serving God. Decapolis is not a city, but a region of ten cities. He told what Jesus had done for him throughout the entire region. Consider what a lifelong task that was, especially without the modern transportation we have today, the communication tools at our disposal, and the means of the printed page. He simply told everyone who would listen what this Man named Jesus had done for him back in those nasty tombs. He told how Jesus had brought him light into the world of darkness he lived in. He told how they too could be delivered from the unclean spirit that controlled them by simply trusting Jesus and following Him.

Why was it so important for this to be recorded about the faithfulness of this one man who trusted Jesus to help him when no other could? If we fast- forward in our Bibles to Mark chapter 7 and verse 31 we find Jesus visiting the coasts of Decapolis. Matthew chapter 15 verse 29 is the parallel account which explains how many were brought to Jesus to be healed and to hear His teaching.

(Matthew 15:29) *And Jesus departed from thence, and came nigh unto the sea of Galilee; and went up into a mountain, and sat down there. (30) And great multitudes came unto him, having with them those that were lame, blind, dumb, maimed, and many others, and cast them down at Jesus' feet; and he healed them: (31) Insomuch that the multitude wondered, when they saw the dumb to speak, the maimed to be whole, the lame to walk, and the blind to see: and they glorified the God of Israel.*

In verse 38 the size of the crowd is recorded, *"And they that did eat were four thousand men, beside women and children."* Not only did Jesus teach them and heal their sick, but He miraculously fed them all with much left over (verses 32-38). Suppose each of the four thousand men had an average family of four with him, a wife and three children. That gives a new dimension to what Jesus did when we consider there could very well have been sixteen to twenty-thousand people there or more, and He fed them all with food to spare. To put this in perspective, that is the number of people we see in some of today's college and professional sports arenas.

How did they all hear about this One named Jesus and what He was doing in their country? Jesus didn't have a team of advance people going to the towns ahead of Him with newspaper articles and radio ads promoting a meeting time and place. He didn't put anything on social media or buy billboard space along the roads and in the towns. And yet great masses of people thronged Him everywhere He went. How did they know?

(Mark 5:20) *And he departed, and began to publish in Decapolis how great things Jesus had done for him: and all men did marvel.*

This is the same man that was running wild through the tombs under the control of the unclean spirit. He became an important part of Jesus' "advance team." When Jesus cast the unclean spirit from the man he became a new creature. He became a servant of the most-high God and he obeyed Jesus' words to go and tell others what had happened to him. He didn't enter any type of training program and he probably didn't know much scripture, if any. All he knew is what Jesus had done for him and he didn't keep it to himself. He told of a deliverance that was complete and immediate; and he made sure everyone knew it was all about Jesus and nothing about himself.

Since you are reading this book there is a great probability that you are struggling under the control of an unclean spirit that has led you to an addiction to something, or you know of someone who is struggling. The total and complete deliverance from any addiction is found by eliminating the source which is the unclean spirit. Until the unclean spirit is dealt with the controlling influence will remain. It may be subdued for a season, but until it is completely eliminated the potential for its controlling influence is always present.

Admitting the source of the addiction to the Lord is the first step. Submitting yourself to Jesus completely is the next. Jesus will remove the unclean spirit and will show you how to keep another from returning through His Word, the Bible. As you read the next chapter you will learn what Jesus requires from you for deliverance to take place.

Chapter 3 How to Have Jesus Cleanse the Unclean Spirit from You

Psalm 51:1-4

Psalms 51:1-4 *Have mercy upon me, O God, according to thy lovingkindness: according unto the multitude of thy tender mercies blot out my transgressions. (2) Wash me throughly from mine iniquity, and cleanse me from my sin. (3) For I acknowledge my transgressions: and my sin is ever before me. (4) Against thee, thee only, have I sinned, and done this evil in thy sight: that thou mightest be justified when thou speakest, and be clear when thou judgest.*

Many years ago, there was a comedian who would use the line, "the devil made me do it" every time he was caught doing something he should not have been doing or saying something he should not have said. While most of his routines were comical, in real life that will not work before a holy and righteous God. You may ask, "Well isn't the devil the root of all of the evil in my life?" While that may be true in that he placed the thoughts and temptations into your mind to start with, the actions which resulted were *your* choice. You can construct any number of scenarios as to "why" you sinned, but the bottom line in all of them is that you chose to sin.

This Psalm was written by King David after he had been confronted by the prophet (God's man in the Old Testament) Nathan with the sin David had committed. David committed adultery with Bathsheba, the wife of one of King David's most loyal soldiers, Uriah. Then he had Uriah murdered in an attempt to cover up his sin. King David did not begin by bringing before God all of the great and mighty things he had done up to that time or the fact that he was the king over God's chosen people. He did not mention to God anything that he had ever done, but began his prayer of confession by seeking the mercy of God.

Psalms 51:1 *Have mercy upon me, O God, ...*

The beginning of forgiveness is *always* God's mercy! It is only through the mercy of God that we can even approach

God in prayer to confess our sin before Him. The word "mercy" basically means "undeserved favor." When a person has committed a very serious crime and the punishment could be great, they will often "throw themselves on the mercy of the court." What they are doing is admitting guilt and asking the court to have sympathy for them by not giving them what they deserve under the law. It is all about God's mercy and never about anything we have ever done.

The attitude among people today when confronted with their sin is to compare themselves with someone else "worse" than they are. "Well, I may have done this, but I am not as bad as he is," seems to be the train of thought that somehow justifies their sin in their eyes. They think God will be impressed with the "smallness" of their sin compared to another person's sin. When a statement like that is made, the one making it does not realize that sin is sin. In God's sight stealing a cookie from the cookie jar when told not to is as "great" of sin as stealing millions of dollars from an elderly person's bank account. Sin is sin. In my work with prisoners I have noticed that it doesn't matter if the crime that was committed was the first one or one of many, the person accused is still locked up in the same cell. It doesn't matter what the person has done with their life to that point, when a law is broken there are consequences to be paid. The only difference is found in the mercy of the Judge.

Psalms 51:1 .... *according unto the multitude of thy tender mercies blot out my transgressions.*

King David is asking God to "blot out" his sin. When a person is sentenced for a crime they have committed it is written in their record; and that record can remain for the rest of their life and be used against them. Someone who has committed crimes of a sexual nature are often required to register as a sex offender for the rest of their life. It is very difficult, if not impossible, to have that removed from the record. However, with God, He not only forgives our sin because of the payment Jesus provided for our sin, but He "blots out" our sin from the eternal record. The action of blotting something out proves that it was written down in the

23

first place. In the "old days" the writing would be blurred or smudged with something to make it unreadable. Today we hit the "delete button" on the computer and it is gone. When we seek God's mercy, based upon Jesus Christ's work on the cross on our behalf, God "hits the delete button" for all eternity. Not because of anything we have ever done, but totally because of God's great mercy to us.

Psalms 51:2 *Wash me throughly from mine iniquity, and cleanse me from my sin.*

Washing is only needed when there is something that is needed to be removed. Dishes are washed because they have food residue on them. Clothes are washed because they have body residue on them. Vehicles are washed because they have road residue on them. We need to be "washed" by God because we have sin residue on us. When I was a kid living at home, one of my chores was to wash the dishes. The standard that was set by my Mom was to wash every dish and every utensil "thoroughly," not just run it through the soapy water a few times. Every speck of food residue must be washed from that dish, otherwise it will contaminate anything good that is placed upon it.

King David is asking God to wash him "thoroughly" so no speck of sins contamination is found in him. He uses two words to describe what he desires God to remove. The word "iniquity" refers to his desire to sin or the process of committing the sin, and the word "sin" is that which deserves the penalty. For instance, as a person is breaking the window to gain entry to a home to rob it, he is desiring to commit a crime. Once he has completed the robbery the crime has been committed. King David wants both removed completely. Not only does he want the penalty for the sin removed but he also wants the desire to commit the sin taken from him.

When an addict attempts to just stop their addictive actions on their own it may work for a time; but unless the *desire* is removed the chances are overwhelming they will return to the addiction. The desire is found in the unclean spirit which communicates with the addict through their thoughts.

The suggestion of how "good" the addictive thing was is once again brought back to the thoughts and as long as it is considered, a return to the addictive action will occur. It is the unclean spirit that must be "washed thoroughly" from the addict and as we saw in the previous chapter only Jesus Christ can do that. How does that happen?

Psalms 51:3 *For I acknowledge my transgressions: and my sin is ever before me.*

The word "acknowledge" means "to know." When we excuse our sin by shifting the blame for it to something or someone else, that is not acknowledging it for what it is. Many people will try to justify their addictive behavior by blaming an abusive or dysfunctional childhood. Others will try to blame their actions on pressure at home, in their marriage, or with rebellious children. Still others will use situations at work to shift the blame upon.

Until it is clearly realized and admitted that the addictive behavior is nothing more than sin it will not be dealt with completely. There must be a humble admission of sin to God. Confessing sin to man is useless and only results in the person who does the confessing feeling good for a time. If another person has been wronged, confession to and forgiveness from that person must be sought when possible. True confession must be made to the One who has been sinned against and that ultimately is God. Notice King David as he wrote his prayer of confession used the word "my" to describe his transgressions (sin). Personal accountability must be taken by the addict, as well as all people, for their choices and resulting actions.

There will be forgiveness from God when sin is humbly admitted to; but there will be consequences. David said, "*my sin is ever before me.*" The consequences are great for an addict and will take time to be worked out in God's plan and will. Remembrance of the sins by the one committing them will always be present and are to be used to keep from going back into that mess. Satan will also use that remembrance to instill doubt of God's forgiveness. However, faith in God's Word and in His unconditional love will squelch that doubt.

Thoughts of unworthiness can be the greatest thoughts Satan will use on an addict to get him or her to return to their addiction. However, there is no place in the Bible where anyone other than Jesus Christ is worthy of God's acceptance. The exact opposite is what is proclaimed throughout scripture. Romans 3:23, *"For all have sinned, and come short of the glory of God."* Romans 3:10 *"As it is written, there is none righteous, no, not one:"* When Satan brings feelings and thoughts of unworthiness, he is actually presenting a truth. No one is worthy regardless of who they are or what they have done. The apostle Paul is a great example of dealing with the thoughts of his past life when he once persecuted the church that he now served.

Philippians 3:13, *"Brethren, I count not myself to have apprehended: but this one thing I do, forgetting those things which are behind, and reaching forth unto those things which are before."*

The thoughts of unworthiness were certainly there since he was doing a great work for the Lord and the opposition from the enemy must have been tremendous. Paul knew exactly who he was in Christ and did not allow his past to interfere with what God's mission was for him in the present.

Psalms 51:4 *Against thee, thee only, have I sinned, and done this evil in thy sight: that thou mightest be justified when thou speakest, and be clear when thou judgest.*

Not only must sin be acknowledged and humbly confessed to God, it must be acknowledged whom the sin has affected. Every addictive behavior has a "victim" and most times there are many. Substance abuse causes the thinking process to be altered, thus their behavior is not what the addict would normally undertake. While under the control of a substance such as drugs or alcohol others can be physically, mentally, and emotionally hurt. Most domestic violence occurs while one or both are under the influence of drugs or alcohol. Those who are participating in the violence are themselves victims; but the children who must endure watching and hearing the conflicts are also victims, often being affected for many years. One who is addicted to pornography victimizes their spouse by violating the vows that they made to be faithful to each other. A person addicted to an explosive temper victimizes everyone he or she explodes upon. The "victim" of an addiction is not limited to just the addict, but all those around him or her are victimized.

Most addicts that become incarcerated and "dry out" have a deep sense of remorse over the things that occurred while under the control of their addiction. I speak with men and women who express a great desire to be with their children and spouses. These are the same children and spouses they neglected for the addictive materials in the first place. There is sorrow over the things that have been lost due to the actions caused by their addictive choices such as family, jobs, houses, vehicles, and of course the large amount of legal fees involved. Often it is extremely difficult to get a meaningful job once their incarceration is completed. To complicate things even more, their driving privileges may be revoked until fines are paid. Addiction is a few moments of "pleasure," but years of struggle and heartache for the addict as well as loved ones.

Before the unclean spirit can be dealt with by Jesus Christ one thing must be clearly seen by the addict. Not only have others been hurt, but it is ultimately God who has been sinned against and offended.

Psalms 51:4 *Against thee, thee only, have I sinned, and done this evil in thy sight...*

While others have been hurt and offended it is against God, and God only, that we have sinned. God has given us everything that we have, including the air we breathe. There is no sin, either thought or deed, that is not known by God.

Isaiah 66: 18, *"For I know their works and their thoughts..."*

Nothing is ever unknown by God and He feels every offense against Him just as we do when someone hurts us. When we think God does not know, or does not care, we deceive ourselves.

Galatians 6:7, *"Be not deceived; God is not mocked: for whatsoever a man soweth, that shall he also reap."*

When a person allows something to control their thoughts and actions other than God they are denying in their hearts that God knows and cares. There can and will be forgiveness and cleansing from God when confession is made to Him admitting that it is He whom the offense has been directed against, but there will also be consequences to be dealt with. Of course, the enemy, Satan, through the unclean spirit will attempt to twist that fact against you. Everything we do in life brings about consequences, good or bad. If you hit your finger with a hammer there *will* be consequences. If you neglect to change the oil in your car, there will be consequences. If you allow anything other than God to control your thoughts and actions, there will be consequences.

Psalms 51:4 *".... that thou mightest be justified when thou speakest, and be clear when thou judgest."*

It must be realized that it is ultimately God's law that has been violated. Violating God's law will often have consequences in man's law as well and there will be penalties to pay. Violating God's law brings loss of blessings as well as loss of fellowship with God. This is not what God desires for anyone; but He is a just God and must deal with people within that justice. God's judgment is not clouded with emotion, but is pure according to His holiness and righteousness.

King David continued on with his prayer of confession in Psalm 51; and I encourage you to prayerfully read and consider what is written. The very first step that must be undertaken in the elimination of the unclean spirit is to humble yourself before God, and admit that it is against Him and Him only that you have sinned. When the thing that is controlling you is thought to be just a habit or something left over from a bad experience, the unclean spirit will remain in charge regardless of the number of "recovery" programs attended or how many prayers are offered. Only Jesus can deal with the unclean spirit that controls you.

Romans 10:9 *That if thou shalt confess with thy mouth the Lord Jesus, and shalt believe in thine heart that God hath raised him from the dead, thou shalt be saved.*

Admitting to God that you are a sinner, that your sin has been directed to Him and Him alone, and humbly asking for His forgiveness through Jesus Christ Who paid the price for all of your sin with His sinless blood will result in that forgiveness being granted by God. God owes you nothing, but gives you everything when you humble yourself before Him and ask for His cleansing.

Chapter 4   How to Avoid Being Entrapped by an Unclean Spirit

Ephesians 4:27-32

Ephesians 4:27-32 *Neither give place to the devil. (28) Let him that stole steal no more: but rather let him labour, working with his hands the thing which is good, that he may have to give to him that needeth. (29) Let no corrupt communication proceed out of your mouth, but that which is good to the use of edifying, that it may minister grace unto the hearers. (30) And grieve not the holy Spirit of God, whereby ye are sealed unto the day of redemption. (31) Let all bitterness, and wrath, and anger, and clamour, and evil speaking, be put away from you, with all malice: (32) And be ye kind one to another, tenderhearted, forgiving one another, even as God for Christ's sake hath forgiven you.*

It has been said that the best cure is prevention. Anyone who has ever been controlled by something undesirable will agree that the worst thing they ever did was to make that first wrong choice. The worst drink of alcohol was the first one. The worst cigarette ever smoked was the first one. The worst hit of drugs was the first one. Had the first one not been chosen, there would be no need to deal with the consequences. Every addict can recall "the first," and every addict is puzzled as to why that choice was made. Where did the temptation come from? How was the door opened for the unclean spirit to enter? There is not a person who does not realize that addictions have terrible, and often deadly consequences. With that knowledge why is the choice made to "do the first one"?

Ephesians 4:27 *Neither give place to the devil.*

The word "place" according to Webster's Dictionary of American English 1828 means "any portion or space marked off; opportunity, power, occasion for acting." When we give "place" to something we designate a place or space for it to occupy. When we "give place to the devil" we are allowing the thoughts that the unclean spirit of the devil gives us to be considered. We give them "space" in our minds. As I have worked with men and women who are incarcerated over the years many of them are drug addicts. I remember one young man who was with us at the county jail and then sentenced to a term in a state prison. Throughout his time of incarceration, he continued with the Bible study lessons from the Prison Discipleship Ministry, and did a good job with them. He seemed to have learned many things and made some very good decisions along the way. A year or so after he was released he was back at the county jail, and I asked him what happened. He told me there was not one day that he did not think about drugs and "getting high" during his entire time of incarceration. He then informed me that the very day he was released he "did drugs."

What happened to the things he learned through the Bible studies and his decisions he made for Christ? Was that all in vain and just something to appease the chaplain? Certainly not since God's Word declares in Isaiah 55:11, *"So shall my word be that goeth forth out of my mouth: it shall not return unto me void, but it shall accomplish that which I please, and it shall prosper in the thing whereto I sent it."* So, what was it that actually happened in the life of this young man to bring about what appeared to be a failure? The key was that he gave place to the devil by taking the thoughts that the unclean spirit was feeding him and allowing them to remain and be attractive to him. Can this happen even to a believer? Absolutely!

God's Word is so very precious and so complete in providing us with everything we need to live a life pleasing to Him, and showing us where the enemy will attack. In Ephesians 4 verses 28 through 32 God gives us the exact areas where Satan will sneak the unclean spirit into our lives. While it is true we cannot stop the thoughts from coming, it is also true that we do not need to give them a "place." We previously illustrated this principle by pointing out that we cannot prevent someone from ringing our doorbell; but we sure have the choice as to who we let in to drink coffee with.

Ephesians 4:28 *Let him that stole steal no more: but rather let him labour, working with his hands the thing which is good, that he may have to give to him that needeth.*

The first area where the unclean spirit tries to get entry into our minds is through our choices. When I was in high school I had a teacher who was somewhat of a philosopher and always seemed to have something very profound to interject into a situation. One day he told us there were two ways of doing anything. Of course, we all thought he was going to say the right way and the wrong way since he was a teacher. When he said the hard way and the easy way it took us all by surprise; but he was totally correct. There is always a hard way and an easy way to most of life's situations. Every one of us have the choice between stealing what we desire or working for it. While stealing may seem to be the easy way, it eventually will be realized that it in fact was the hard way when the consequences are considered. There is a hard way and an easy way when dealing with our emotions and life's situations. We can seek solutions from God's Word and through Christian counsellors or we can take mind altering substances and forget the whole mess for a time. Too often the choice is made to withdraw into our addiction (pornography, temper, etc.) and forget the problems temporarily. The unclean spirit will always make sure those "options" are clearly presented to our stressed mind.

A second area of choice is "me or others," otherwise known as selfishness. How will my actions affect me as well as others? As was mentioned previously, all actions have consequences, either for good or for evil. Will my decision to listen to and act out on the thoughts of the unclean spirit affect me in a desired way while hurting others? Or will my decision benefit others possibly at the cost of my convenience? Choosing to allow the unclean spirit to control you is a very selfish act and will usually cause hurt or injury to others. Consider what the eternal consequences would have been for us if Jesus had listened to the devil when he tempted Him to choose Himself over God in Matthew 4. There would be no salvation and every human being that ever lived would be eternally lost. The choices we make will either open the door to the unclean spirit or will shut it out.

Ephesians 4:29 *Let no corrupt communication proceed out of your mouth, but that which is good to the use of edifying, that it may minister grace unto the hearers.*

The next area where God's Word shows us that the unclean spirit can enter our thoughts is in the area of pride. We all must communicate with ourselves, others, and with God; but there is good communication that honors God as well as "corrupt" communication that gives place to the unclean spirit. "Corrupt" means worthless.

When someone makes a mistake, too often we feel it is our "God-given duty" to correct them, and in doing so shame them and make them feel embarrassed. The root of that attitude is an unclean spirit communicating with you and you listening to it. The words that come out of our mouth are the product of what is in our heart. When self is the object of our heart, mostly selfish words will proceed out of our mouth. When the words out of our mouth are self-serving and self-motivated we are placing ourselves as greater than those around us. Our "God-given duty" is never to tear someone else down, but to build them up or edify them.

If anyone had the "right" to tear down everyone He came in contact with it would have been Jesus. He *was* better than all others; but His attitude and the words that came from His mouth were all words of love even while correcting wrongs. He used strong words at times when needing to correct or admonish deep seated sin, but the motive of His heart was love for that person.

One example was just after His resurrection when He met Mary. She was very discouraged that her loving Saviour Jesus had been crucified, and also very confused when she discovered His body was not in the tomb as it had been. In John 20 verse 16 Jesus simply spoke her name, "Mary," and immediately her grief turned to joy. Jesus could have ripped her up one side and down the other with harsh words for her confusion and ignorance in not understanding what had just happened. Jesus had spoken openly concerning His death and how after three days He would rise from the dead. What was her problem? Why didn't she understand what was going on here? Maybe by admonishing her for her ignorance she would somehow make a greater effort to learn these things. Maybe this would finally convince her that He really was the Son of God. In the end what good would have come out of such a course of action on Jesus' behalf? Absolutely no good and much evil.

I can picture the tone of voice and the voice inflection that Jesus used when speaking her name. "Mary." That was the kind, loving, compassionate voice she had known before the crucifixion which now drew her and comforted her. That is the "tone of voice" Jesus has with each one of us when we mess up and fall. That is the tone we should have with others. Notice the word "no" in Ephesians 4:29. There should be absolutely no time or situation where prideful, self-serving communication, which is entirely and always evil, is to come from our mouth. None! Why is this? It is because the root or source of all evil communication comes from heeding the unclean spirit, and always results in pride.

When pride is present it grows like mold on bread in a dark, damp place. It can begin with a simple "sharp" word to a spouse or a child, and if not checked will grow because our flesh, our sinful nature, loves being in control. From that sharp word in the morning will come sharp words for the person who is tailgating you on the way to work. The work day only fuels the prideful attitude with several opportunities to display your superiority to others. The commute home finds the same tailgater accompanying you as you bark out words of instruction on how to drive, all inside the safety of your car of course.

Upon entering your house, you kick the cat, demand supper be ready now, and stomp off to the man cave, or any place where you can be left alone and take something to "calm you down." This is beginning to feel really good; so, the attitude of superiority is expanded to include God by ignoring what He has shown you is true and correct. After all, one hit on the drugs or one drink never hurt anyone is your reasoning. Just like that, several addictions are launched and are in full bloom. The first is the addiction to "pride," the second is an addiction to an explosive temper, and the third is the addiction to the substance that "makes you feel better about it all."

And it all began with one "sharp" word in the morning. *Let no corrupt communication proceed out of your mouth, but that which is good to the use of edifying, that it may minister grace unto the hearers.* Had that sharp word been a word of loving correction or admonishing, the entire day would have been different and the birth of the addictions would have been averted. The tailgater would have still been there; but instead of yelling "instructions" to them you would have prayed for them. Much would have been accomplished at work with fellow workers being encouraged to think beyond their situations and consider the working of God in their lives. Then prayer for the tailgater on the way home, kiss the spouse, pet the cat, and patiently wait for supper while reading your Bible and meditating on the goodness of God that day. What an impact a few simple words can have on an entire day!

Ephesians 4:30 *And grieve not the holy Spirit of God, whereby ye are sealed unto the day of redemption.*

This verse shows that stubbornness can also be an entryway for the unclean spirit to become a consideration in our lives. The word "grieve" means to make sorrowful or to offend. When we stubbornly ignore the leadership and guidance of the Holy Spirit we find ourselves with the attitude so often found in children; "my way" or the classic "it's mine." Constantly insisting on our way or on our possessions when the Holy Spirit is clearly guiding in a different direction is stubbornness which comes from heeding the unclean spirit. Stubbornness and pride go hand in hand to combine in producing an attitude that eventually will eliminate the influence and direction of the Holy Spirit in our life.

When I think of stubbornness I think of a wild horse who in its stubbornness proclaims that it will not be ridden under any circumstances, and bucks off anyone who tries. Until the stubbornness of the horse is broken it will be useless to its owner. When we continuously "buck off" the Holy Spirit we are useless to the One who created us for His purpose. The stubbornness which is manifest in our hearts and lives brings grief to the Holy Spirit just as it does to the one who tries over and over to break the wild horse without any success. Instead of the Holy Spirit being the source of guidance in our life, self becomes our object and the unclean spirit is busy pumping thoughts into our mind that go contrary to God's will.

When stubbornness and pride gather momentum, the result will be a controlling addiction which is the entire aim of the unclean spirit. The controlling addiction may not be substance abuse, but may show itself in an explosive temper, over-indulging in such things as eating, sleeping, entertainment, or any number of things which control us in place of the Holy Spirit of God. The simple solution is to "grieve not the Holy Spirit" by allowing Him to identify the unclean spirit in your life and turning from it.

Ephesians 4:31 *Let all bitterness, and wrath, and anger, and clamour, and evil speaking, be put away from you, with all malice:*

Our world today is filled with *"bitterness, wrath, anger, clamour* (loudness), *and evil speaking."* All one needs to do is watch an innocent baseball game or football game on television and observe the content of the commercials. How many times within the few minutes of commercials is your mind bombarded with killing, violence, evil speaking, loudness, nudity, cheating, whether real or animated, and all manner of God-dishonoring things? The football game almost seems "tame" compared to the content of most commercials!

All of this demonstrates an attitude the world is trying to force upon the population. As these things are watched over and over the unclean spirit within us is gaining ground and soon we either give in to their message or we become complacent about it all. The attitude you have towards something will determine the action you take regarding it. When the unclean spirit represents evil as good, it is trying to get you to fall.

We are to put it away from us, which means that we are to actively move it out of our minds and from our presence. It is impossible to live in this world and not be subjected to the workings of an unclean spirit in others. Those who promote evil are themselves under the control of an unclean spirit without knowing and often without caring as long as their desires are fulfilled. Many years ago, when our children were young we took them to Disney World in Florida. There was a ride at that time which took you past a mirror as you exited and turned the car you were riding in so you faced the mirror. To everyone's amusement as they looked in the mirror they saw themselves; but also next to them was the image of a friendly "hitchhiker." It was a skeleton with a smile and with his bag packed leaving the ride with you. While this was a great effect produced by Disney World, there is a certain amount of truth connected with it. When we take the "ride" through an "attraction" that is not God-honoring the chances are we will come out of it with an unwanted and unseen "hitchhiker," an unclean spirit. The proof of the presence of the unclean spirit is the desire to partake of the "attraction" again.

Not only is this true of every addiction, the thing that controls you, but it is more easily seen in an addiction to pornography. When illicit scenes are viewed it brings a few moments of satisfaction, but within a very short period of time the unclean spirit begins to make its case for more. As a person indulges themselves, the time of satisfaction gets shorter and shorter until it is non-existent. The thing that takes the viewer away from what they are looking at is either a tremendous sense of guilt or they are interrupted by someone or something that causes them to shut it off. The "hitchhiker," the unclean spirit, is still there and constantly in the background spilling thoughts into the mind to be on the look-out for the next encounter.

An addiction to pornography is certainly not limited to the use of the internet or magazines. The person that is addicted to pornographic and sexual things will be looking for the opportunity to fulfil his lust anywhere he can. It may be something as simple and brief as a lady bent over fastening a child into a car seat in a parking lot who is scantily dressed. It may be a suggestive billboard on the commute to work, or the secretary who needs to cover herself up more modestly. Those small "shots" will keep the sexual addict in an attitude of always wanting more and never being satisfied enough to turn completely away.

This is true with every addiction regardless of what the nature of it is. When something attempts to control you, the opportunities will always present themselves for you to indulge. Since we are seemingly emerged in opportunities, how do we fulfil the command to *"put away from you"*? The first thing needed is an attitude adjustment towards the unclean spirit that is desiring to control you. Recognizing the source of the wrong thoughts is a giant step in eliminating them from your life. I have ministered to many who are addicted to something and when it is realized that the source of all of their desire begins with something as simple as a thought, they are totally amazed.

I was speaking with a man who has an addiction to cocaine about the source of his addiction being that first thought from the unclean spirit. When he processed what I was showing him in his mind he was totally amazed at the simplicity of it all in the beginning; and the control that one thought had led to in his life. By him not *"putting away"* from him, but allowing that thought to remain, he caved in to peer pressure and took his first drugs into his body. As I spoke with him, he is incarcerated and possibly facing some prison time for his actions while under the control of those drugs. His family has left him, he will be difficult to employ when he is released, and his life is at the bottom, all of that while in his mid-thirties. As the realization of how it all began with allowing one thought from an unclean spirit to remain in his mind, he acted as if a great light had just been turned on in his heart which clearly revealed the truth.

Not only are we commanded to *"put away from you"* the things listed in verse 31, but it guides us how we are to do it. The word *"malice"* means having the desire to do something with no regard to the consequences or injury caused to self or others. In other words, make an attitude adjustment concerning the thoughts presented by the unclean spirit. Desire only comes from exposure to something. For example, if you set a chocolate candy bar on the desk next to me it would not be too long before my desire would be to move it from the desk to my stomach. However, if I took it and placed it in the desk drawer, way in the back, the chances are I would not have thoughts about it. But even better would be to never allow the chocolate bar to be brought into my office in the first place. That may be a crude illustration, but I think you get my point. If you have an addiction issue do not favor it by knowingly placing yourself in a position for the unclean spirit to prompt you to take action. Your attitude towards the thought from the unclean spirit will determine the outcome and prevent it from entering your life in the first place.

Ephesians 4:32 *And be ye kind one to another, tenderhearted, forgiving one another, even as God for Christ's sake hath forgiven you.*

We live in a world that is filled with violence and hatred. I feel very qualified to boldly make that statement since most of my childhood was during the 1950's. I remember that as being a time when people generally were kind one to another and went out of their way to help regardless of the cost. People we did not agree with were still respected as people, and our convictions about the things of God were strong and apparent. Comparing those times with the world today is a frightening thing especially realizing the direction society is going.

Another proof of the change in the attitude of society is the presence of "security officers" in our elementary schools. Teachers with concealed carry permits having weapons in the classroom for protection was something not even dreamed of just a few years ago, but today is a common as well as a needed thing. One of the men that volunteers in our jail chapel ministry is the director of security for our local school system and he is amazed at the changes he has seen in the attitudes and behavior of not only students but parents. Our society has become a "me first" society; and that has happened as the unclean spirit is allowed to be present in the mind of the majority of people.

The area of forgiveness is a major area where the unclean spirit will enter if we are not constantly on guard. It is so very easy today to demand *our* rights at the expense of someone else. What if Jesus had held that attitude? What if Jesus said, "This isn't right! I demand that my rights be recognized and things be done my way. After all, I am God!" The result would be that none of us would ever be saved and payment in full of our sin debt would be demanded from each one of us. Jesus allowed Himself to be placed in a position of cruel punishment to the point of death for the sins of others. He is the portrayal of ultimate kindness, tenderheartedness, and forgiveness and should be the standard we look to in our lives.

When a person demands their "rights" when they are opposed and they leave a confrontation with an unkind and unforgiving spirit, the door is wide open for the unclean spirit to place every conceivable thought into their mind. Murders have been committed as a result of the unclean spirit's relentless thoughts being heeded. Domestic violence has happened as the unclean spirit presses for revenge within the thoughts of the one wronged. Substance abuse and all forms of addiction have begun as a result of an unforgiving attitude which is allowed to remain and fester.

The definition of "forgiveness" is "to pardon; to give graciously, give freely; bestow." Notice the one word that runs through that definition. It is the word "give." Forgiveness is giving of yourself to others by giving up what you believe to be your rights for the good of another. Forgiveness is offering an apology even when you feel it was not your fault. Forgiving is looking beyond your desires and seeing others' needs for comfort and love. Forgiving is the product of listening to and obeying the *clean* spirit, the Spirit of God, as opposed to the *unclean* spirit.

Forgiveness is the foundation upon which kindness and tenderheartedness are built. There can be no kindness without forgiveness. Forgiveness does not come naturally to man since the sin nature within him is rooted in the thoughts presented by the unclean spirit. This spirit comes from Satan's demons communicating with our mind.

Chapter 5   How to Stay Free from the Unclean Spirit's Control

Philippians 3:12-14; Hebrews 10:25

Philippians 3:12-14 *Not as though I had already attained, either were already perfect: but I follow after, if that I may apprehend that for which also I am apprehended of Christ Jesus. (13) Brethren, I count not myself to have apprehended: but this one thing I do, forgetting those things which are behind, and reaching forth unto those things which are before, (14) I press toward the mark for the prize of the high calling of God in Christ Jesus.*

It is a wonderful and amazing thing when a person who has struggled so intensely under the control of an unclean spirit, and the addiction that follows, is finally set free. The voice in your thoughts is finally overcome and is silenced, or is no longer a controlling factor. The work of Jesus is never partial and deliverance from the unclean spirit is complete. However, there are still pitfalls that must be realized and avoided.

The beginning part of these verses presents the main reason a person allows the unclean spirit to re-enter their thoughts; with a return to the controlling addiction soon to follow. The verse begins with the words, *"Not as though I had already attained, either were already perfect."* When newly found freedom is realized as a part of their life confidence begins to build. When that confidence is placed properly in Jesus Christ and Him alone the unclean spirit has no chance. However, when confidence is placed in self to be able to "keep clean," the door has begun to open for the return of the unclean spirit. Over the years, I have had it told to me by those who had experienced freedom from addiction that they thought they "could handle it" and began to come in close contact with the elements of the addiction they once knew. I have had those who were alcoholics but freed from that bondage tell me how they would go to a party and think "just one drink to be social would not hurt." Quicker than they could realize the unclean spirit had returned in full force; and the controlling addiction had returned, often worse than before.

As long as we live we will *never* arrive at a place where *we* can be the one who can handle the unclean spirit. All one needs to do is observe their own track record and see how their "handling it" didn't work out too well. Looking at others who thought they could "handle it" is also proof that it doesn't work, and only opens the door for the unclean spirit to sneak back in. Once it is allowed in it begins to grow like mold on cheese, very rapidly. Back in chapter one we looked at the man with the unclean spirit and how *"no man could tame him"* (Mark 5:4). That included the man himself. If he could have done something to "handle" the unclean spirit in his life he certainly would have, but instead we see him *"crying and cutting himself with stones"* (Mark 5:5).

The apostle Paul is the human writer of the book of Philippians which he penned under holy inspiration of God. That giant of the faith is writing that he had not arrived at the point where he could handle temptations given by the unclean spirit, the thoughts that Satan and his demons place in our minds.

Philippians 3:12 *Not as though I had already attained, either were already perfect: but I follow after, if that I may apprehend that for which also I am apprehended of Christ Jesus."*

He states that he does not consider himself perfect or that he in any way can handle things, *"but I follow after."* Who or what is he following after? He makes it very clear he is not following after his imperfect wisdom, but rather is following after Jesus Christ. *"...but I follow after, if that I may apprehend* [understand] *that for which also I am apprehended* [understood] *of Christ Jesus."* In other words, Paul follows Jesus so he can know what it is that Jesus thinks of him; the way he truly is. Paul does not want anything that would sidetrack him in his life for Christ such as following his own direction. One of the deadliest things a person can do is to follow what they think is right and what they think they can handle without first consulting with God and His Word.

As we observed in Mark 5:13 only Jesus can direct the unclean spirit out of our lives. We can certainly let it in; but only Jesus can get it out. By following Jesus and His leadership we can avoid the situations where the unclean spirit can make its entrance. Many have told me that as long as they were following Christ, their life was totally clean from the addiction they faced. When they thought they would be okay without Jesus in their life everything went back to where it had been, or worse.

Philippians 3:13-14 *Brethren, I count not myself to have apprehended: but this one thing I do, forgetting those things which are behind, and reaching forth unto those things which are before, (14) I press toward the mark for the prize of the high calling of God in Christ Jesus.*

Paul restates that he does not know everything, *"but this one thing I do, forgetting those things which are behind..."* Before the apostle Paul was saved and placed his trust in Jesus Christ he persecuted the church and Christians to the point of death. His past included murder of God's children, Christian believers. One can only imagine how Satan and his demons constantly pursued Paul with the unclean spirit of his past, trying to get him to see his own past sin as something that would disqualify him for the task ahead. As the unclean spirit came to him with accusations of his past he learned that he must forget *"those things which are behind."* The past is the past and there is nothing anyone can do to change it. When it is confessed to God as sin (1 John 1:9) He not only forgives, but forgets and holds nothing against us as believers (Hebrews 8:12).

Every person I meet that is incarcerated and has actually committed a crime tells me that if they could just turn back the clock and had the ability to change things they would. Several years ago, a man named Peter came through the jail and as I got to know him I was able to introduce him to Jesus. He placed his trust in Christ to save him. Peter was in his late fifties and had a past that was less than stellar; but when Peter met Jesus his whole life changed. He didn't let his past discourage him from serving the newly found Saviour with all his heart. He was convicted and given a life sentence with no chance of parole. I spoke with Peter the night before he left for prison and he told me that if he could change things he would in a heartbeat. However, he realized that God is now in control of his life; and he was excited to see what God had ahead for him. I have stayed in touch with Peter and he tells me that his entire purpose in life is still "finding someone he can tell about this One named Jesus he met at Stark County jail."

Peter is living exactly what the apostle Paul wrote in these verses. He learned that in order to forget *"those things which are behind"* one must place something more powerful in its place.

Philippians 3:13-14 .... *forgetting those things which are behind, and reaching forth unto those things which are before, (14) I press toward the mark for the prize of the high calling of God in Christ Jesus.*

In order for the past to be forgotten there must be something to *"reach forth"* unto. When the unclean spirit is removed by Jesus in the life of an addict and he or she begins to follow Christ, they are to look forward to what He has to offer them in the way of blessings, freedom, and a purpose for life. However, when they begin to consider the past and lose sight of where God is leading them, they will once again begin to consider the thoughts that the unclean spirit is tempting them with. All too often they choose to once again listen to those thoughts and slip back into the addiction.

The apostle Paul states that the process of forgetting in his life is a struggle. We see this in the word *"press."* The definition of the word press is "to urge with force or weight" (Webster's Dictionary of American English – 1828). He had to work at following Jesus every moment of every day. He had to bring "force" or "weight" to bear against the unclean spirit to keep it away. Think of it like a chess match between two opponents. One makes a move, and the other must counter the move. When one ceases to make a counter move the game is over and he is defeated. Satan and his demons will make a move into your thoughts with the unclean spirit. In order to

45

remain in a competitive mode there must be a counter move. When there ceases to be a counter move the unclean spirit wins and is allowed to remain as victor. These counter moves cannot be simply from within the person being tempted as a result of self-will, but must be as a result of pressing *"toward the mark for the prize of the high calling of God in Christ Jesus."*

The *"prize"* is a life under the control of the *clean spirit*, the Holy Spirit of God, and not the unclean spirit. You may ask, how is this possible seeing how the unclean spirit has access to our thoughts at any moment? The answer is the same as with any addiction recovery program. One must have a support system around them to keep going in the right direction; as well as something to give encouragement and wisdom when the unclean spirit seems unbearable. God certainly will not allow someone who is genuinely seeking freedom from the control of the unclean spirit to go it on their own. He has provided everything needed for success and it is all attainable within our human capabilities.

Hebrews 10:25 Not *forsaking the assembling of ourselves together, as the manner of some is; but exhorting one another: and so much the more, as ye see the day approaching.*

God never designed man to go it alone. If you think about it, even the <u>Lone</u> Ranger had Tonto, Batman had Robin, but Edward Smith went it alone. Edward Smith? Who is he? That's exactly what I mean; he went it alone and never made it as a "super-hero." Seriously, God shows us in Genesis 2:18 that *"it is not good that man should be alone."* God knew that when man is alone he is vulnerable to the attacks of Satan through the unclean spirit. When someone who has been released from the control of an addiction by Jesus thinks they can continue to fight off the unclean spirit on their own, it is an insult to the work Jesus has done in their life. It was Jesus alone that delivered them. What makes them think that they can then handle what they could not handle in the first place now? God, the One who created man, knows everything that makes him a person; and God shows us that it is not good for man to be alone.

Jesus has provided the greatest "support group" man could ever need by establishing the church. As I have worked with those incarcerated I stress three things that are absolutely essential to keep them from relapse. First is God's Word which they need to be reading, thinking about, and applying to their lives every day. Second is prayer which is the communication link between them and their heavenly Father; and should include talking to God about everything. Third is church involvement. Don't just pick a church on any corner and go there; but seek out a church where the Bible and only the Bible is the rule of guidance and teaching. All churches are not the same, as most people have been led to believe by the unclean spirit who does not want the true Word of God to be a strong influence. Church involvement is the one area most neglected by most people that I minister to. That is like someone with a medical issue consulting with a doctor, filling the prescription for the medicine prescribed, but never taking it, and then claiming that it "didn't work for them."

A Bible teaching, Bible-believing church is not a place where man's opinions are intertwined with God's Word. When anything is added to or taken away from God's Word it stops being truth and becomes a lie (Revelation 22:18-19). The church is a place for encouragement and comfort centered around Jesus among those who attend. The church is not a place where people judge one another for anything including their past, their appearance, or the color of their skin. If that is taking place in a so-called church, it ceases to be a church and becomes a social organization from God's standpoint.

I have found that most people hesitate going to a church because of fear that they will not "fit in." Fear is not of God and comes totally from the unclean spirit. Consider the motives of the unclean spirit in not wanting a person who has been delivered from under its control to be in a place where strength and wisdom are given. By finding "excuses" not to become involved with God's church the person is playing right back into the purpose of the unclean spirit. Why would the impulse to <u>not</u> go to church be so very strong if it were not something that could keep the unclean spirit out?

Every addict has a "leader" that they follow. The drug addict has a dealer; the alcoholic has the liquor store; the porn addict has the internet; the over-eater has the grocery store; and the person with an explosive temper has his own pride and self-gratification. Those who are "addicted" to Jesus and the church have the Pastor. God has already placed people in positions of leadership within His church just to minister to the needs of the people.

Ephesians 4:11-12 *And he gave some, apostles; and some, prophets; and some, evangelists; and some, pastors and teachers; (12) For the perfecting [maturing] of the saints, for the work of the ministry, for the edifying [encouraging] of the body of Christ:*

I have pastored and have been involved with many churches over the years as interim pastor; and I can honestly tell you that I never had the need or desire to follow the people around all week just to see what I needed to preach about. All the Pastor and the teachers in the church need to do for direction is submit themselves to God; and He will lead in the exact direction every person attending is in need of hearing. God will meet your need for victory over the unclean spirit through His church; but you cannot receive that victory without going and being consistent.

We have someone better than the Lone Ranger's Tonto and Batman's Robin. We have the God of all creation guiding us step-by-step to defeat the controlling influence of the unclean spirit in our lives if we will simply and humbly submit to Him. It is the same God who created the billions and billions of stars in the universe; that created all of the working systems in the tiniest bug on the planet; and that knows and cares for the innermost thoughts you have, who will use the Pastor and teachers who humble themselves before Him to give you exactly what God wants you to hear and act upon.

1 Corinthians 1:21 *For after that in the wisdom of God the world by wisdom knew not God, it pleased God by the foolishness of preaching to save them that believe.*

God has chosen to use man to reveal Himself to mankind. While there are some that seek their own gain, most men that pastor Bible teaching churches are men that God uses to show you exactly what you need. Spiritual growth and preventing the unclean spirit from returning and controlling you can only be had by putting all three of the "tools" God has provided into active use in your life. Bible reading and applying what you learn, prayer, and church involvement are the three keys in God's plan.

Two out of three in any area of life falls short of the goal. If a doctor prescribes a medicine to be taken three times a day and the patient only take it two out of three, the results will be less than expected. If you show up for work two out of three days you will probably be soon looking for employment. Bible reading, prayer, and church are the three ingredients God has prescribed for a growing and vibrant faith. Two out of three will produce results less than desirable, with a great chance that the unclean spirit will make a return and control. Be diligent about following God's leadership to the "right" church He has chosen for you. Finding the "best" in anything is always worth the search.

Chapter 6   What Happens When We "Slip"?

1 John 1:5-10

1 John 1:5-10 *This then is the message which we have heard of him, and declare unto you, that God is light, and in him is no darkness at all. (6) If we say that we have fellowship with him, and walk in darkness, we lie, and do not the truth: (7) But if we walk in the light, as he is in the light, we have fellowship one with another, and the blood of Jesus Christ his Son cleanseth us from all sin. (8) If we say that we have no sin, we deceive ourselves, and the truth is not in us. (9) If we confess our sins, he is faithful and just to forgive us our sins, and to cleanse us from all unrighteousness. (10) If we say that we have not sinned, we make him a liar, and his word is not in us.*

Serving God as a jail chaplain as well as the director of the Prison Discipleship Ministry is the most exciting thing I have ever been given the opportunity to do in my many years in the ministry. Not knowing what God has planned for a day is thrilling; but would be very scary if it were not for the fact that God loves me and uses me to accomplish His purpose which is telling others about the marvellous, unconditional gift of love and forgiveness provided through His Son Jesus Christ.

My ministry assignment at the jail is especially exciting when I pull onto the property in the morning and see one or more law enforcement vehicles transporting prisoners *into* the jail. God is bringing another load to visit with me for a time, and I have another bunch of precious souls to share Jesus with. Where a Pastor must go out and try to encourage people to come to church, all I need do is show up and God brings them to me. It certainly does not get any better than that!

1 John 1:5 *This then is the message which we have heard of him, and declare unto you, that God is light, and in him is no darkness at all.*

God has one message to the addict and that message is, "*God is light.*" When a person who has been in the sunlight comes into a totally dark room their vision is plunged into the darkness; and moving around that room is very hazardous. What they need is light because light dispels darkness. When you go into a dark room the only thing that will get the darkness out is light. The only thing that will get the darkness of the unclean spirit out of the mind is the light of God, because "*God is light.*" God is totally light and "*in Him is no darkness at all*" which means that all of the darkness is driven out by the presence of God in a person's life.

Contrary to most people's thinking, God has no evil, dark thoughts towards anyone, including the addict. He will not bring evil consequences upon you as a part of His "revenge" upon you for your sin. What He does allow into your life are situations where you will be able to see the corrections needed by His illuminating light of the Holy Spirit.

Jeremiah 29:11 *For I know the thoughts that I think toward you, saith the LORD, thoughts of peace, and not of evil, to give you an expected end.*

The "expected end" God wants you to see and know is His love, His peace, and His forgiveness.

1 John 1:6 *If we say that we have fellowship with him, and walk in darkness, we lie, and do not the truth:*

As I visit with inmates and get to know them I find many have a church background, but have regrettably chosen to walk away from God. They see what has taken place in their lives; and most are looking for the way back to a good relationship with the Lord. However, there are those who do not yet see their need for that relationship. As I go through the housing areas and sign up men and women for one of the thirteen chapel services we conduct each week I have some who tell me, "No Chap. I'm alright." There is that element within me that wants to ask them why they think they are "alright" when they are on the inside of the bars and wearing an orange jumpsuit; but I am gracious and offer what help they may seek down the road.

Probably the most destructive message the unclean spirit can plant in one's thoughts is that they are "alright." The unclean spirit brings nothing but darkness into the heart and soul of a person who allows it to remain. Anything that controls a person other than the Holy Spirit of God only produces darkness. When the unclean spirit convinces its host that the darkness is "alright" is when it begins to control. I receive letters from many inmates who have made good decisions in their lives to follow Christ and seek His guidance both while they are incarcerated and when they are released. Some write that they will "never go back to that again," whatever "that" was in their life. My response to them is always one of caution because it is not *if* they will slip, but *when*. The person who allows the unclean spirit to remain for any amount of time in their thoughts is already on the first step of a fall back into problems.

Going through life with a tee shirt on with the name of Jesus on it or listening to "Christian" music while still indulging in their addiction is not fellowship with God, but a lie from the unclean spirit. The key word in verse six is the word "walk." We can talk the talk all day long, but if we do not walk the walk we are deceiving ourselves. God's Word tells us to be *"doers of the Word, and not hearers only, deceiving our own selves"* (James 1:22).

Walking in darkness means that you are content to continue in your sin. You have an attitude that everything is alright between you and others', between you and God; and even between you and yourself. Regardless of how much you pray or partake of "religious" things, God's Word boldly and plainly states that as long as you are content to continue in your addiction, or any sin, you are a liar and what you are doing is not truth.

1 John 1:7 *But if we walk in the light, as he is in the light, we have fellowship one with another, and the blood of Jesus Christ his Son cleanseth us from all sin.*

Walking in the light happens when you are walking in the path that Jesus has given you regardless of what you think or how you feel about it. Walking in the light will produce the desire to be around other believers and have fellowship one with another. The reason for this is because of the blood of Jesus which has done the same work in those you associate with as it did in you. Verse 7 does not just state that the blood of Jesus saves us from all sin; but it goes further and shows that it also cleanses us from all sin. When something is "cleansed" every last bit of what caused the stain or filth is removed. If only part of the grease were removed from a mechanics shirt it would not be considered "clean" and would still be considered dirty. It is the same with our sin. Jesus' blood has completely cleansed us from sin.

1 John 1:8-9 *If we say that we have no sin, we deceive ourselves, and the truth is not in us. (9) If we confess our sins, he is faithful and just to forgive us our sins, and to cleanse us from all unrighteousness.*

Each one of us has a choice concerning our sin. We can either chose to deny that it exists (verse 8) or we can admit to God that it is sin (verse 9). Each choice has a different outcome so a careful choice is extremely important. Saying we have no sin, or that our sin is not as bad as it could be or as bad as others, results in deceiving ourselves. It is like looking in the mirror at yourself and denying that what you see really is there. There are no gray hairs, no wrinkles, no extra pounds, and you imagine yourself as you once were. Reality shows you that you are getting older and changing. The reality of your addiction, or any sin, is that it is sin.

As we have seen in previous chapters sin has real consequences regardless if we admit to it or not. The unclean spirit will not help you make the correct decision because it will place thoughts in your mind that "if you really were a Christian you would not have done that." The guilt you experience will only serve to drive you deeper into your addiction and farther away from God until you bring it to God admitting that it is sin.

Confessing means that you agree with someone regarding something. When a person commits a crime and they "confess" to it, they are admitting that what they are accused of is what happened and they are guilty. When a believer confesses his or her sin to God they are admitting that what they did was indeed sin, and they are seeking God's forgiveness for it. It is through the faithfulness and justice of God alone that forgiveness is granted on the basis of what Jesus has done on the cross. God does not just stop with forgiveness, but also cleanses from that sin.

What happens when we "slip" and fall back into what we have left behind? Don't stay in that sin; but immediately take it to God, and humbly admit what you have done. Remaining in it will only cause more guilt and that downward spiral which leads back to the control of the unclean spirit in your life. Confession must also be linked to repentance. A very simple definition of repentance is "to run in the opposite direction." As you were heading towards the addictive thing, confess it to God and run towards Him. Continuing in sin will cause you to stop reading the Bible, stop praying effectively, and will stop your desire to be with God's people. It is a battle for control of your mind; and the one who wins is the one you choose to win by your decisions and actions.

We all have seen a small child try to walk and fall down. While there may be a certain amount of crying involved, the bottom line is that the child must get back up and try again; otherwise there is something terribly wrong. The falls in a child's life are all a part of learning and are expected. The same is true with a believer regardless of how long or short they have been saved. "Falls" are a part of growing and learning and are God's way of strengthening and maturing our faith. Certain trouble comes when the person is content to lay there and whine instead of getting up and going again.

1 John 1:9 *If we confess our sins, he is faithful and just to forgive us our sins, and to cleanse us from all unrighteousness.*

Chapter 7 Why a Storm?

The Church's Part in an Addict's Life

Mark 4:35-41

Mark 4:35-41 *And the same day, when the even was come, he saith unto them, Let us pass over unto the other side. (36) And when they had sent away the multitude, they took him even as he was in the ship. And there were also with him other little ships. (37) And there arose a great storm of wind, and the waves beat into the ship, so that it was now full. (38) And he was in the hinder part of the ship, asleep on a pillow: and they awake him, and say unto him, Master, carest thou not that we perish? (39) And he arose, and rebuked the wind, and said unto the sea, Peace, be still. And the wind ceased, and there was a great calm. (40) And he said unto them, Why are ye so fearful? how is it that ye have no faith? (41) And they feared exceedingly, and said one to another, What manner of man is this, that even the wind and the sea obey him?*

Why has this happened to me? That is probably the question I hear the most in my ministering to those who are incarcerated as well as people in general. They are looking at the circumstances instead of what Jesus is doing in their lives to guide them and direct them into His perfect plan for their lives. When I was a child I was terrified of thunder and lightning storms; but now I am fascinated with the beauty of the lightning and the power of the sound of thunder. What made the difference? Understanding what a storm actually is, and that it represents a part of God's creation removes the terror and makes it marvellous to behold. What about the "storms" of life? How can they ever be marvellous when they usually bring elements into our lives that we would rather not have? Is there a purpose for the "storms" of life? Is there a way that we can escape them?

In Mark 4:35-41 the Word of God gives us an account of a physical storm that came upon Jesus and His disciples. Through this account we can see many principles that will help us understand what God may be trying to accomplish in our lives when the "storms" of life come upon us.

Mark 4:35 *And the same day, when the even was come, he saith unto them, Let us pass over unto the other side.*

In the previous verses of chapter four we learn that Jesus had been teaching a crowd of people throughout the entire day. He was in the area of Capernaum on the shore of the Sea of Galilee. The people were standing or sitting on the shore, and Jesus was in a fishing vessel which was pushed out from the shore so all could hear Him. This had the effect of an amphitheater. As the day was ending Jesus instructed the disciples that He wanted to go to the other side of the Sea of Galilee. In Jesus' instructions He used the word "us" which meant not only were they going, but He was going also. When we embark on the journey of our daily endeavors it is Jesus, through the power of the Holy Spirit, who is there with us instructing us as we go. Notice there was no specific destination given by Jesus, only the fact that they were going "*unto the other side.*"

By giving this instruction Jesus was telling the disciples that they were not staying where they were but were going to another place. Jesus does not want us as individuals to remain in the same situations we are in; but we are to be constantly growing our faith in Him. This instruction is also to the church. The mission of the church can be summed up in the words "take Jesus to the other side." The church is to take Jesus "over there," wherever "over there" may be. Too many times the church folks lose sight of that mission and begin to reason within themselves as the disciples possibly did.

I can almost picture Peter letting Jesus know that there was no need to go "over there" since there was a great multitude right here. The people were very receptive and were learning much, so what was the point of leaving all of this and going "over there"? While that is not written in the text we are considering, human nature would tell us that someone was at least thinking it. The sad thing is that when the attitude of keeping things just as they are when Jesus wants us to take Him "over there" is adopted, our faith stagnates and the church becomes an organization instead of the church Jesus built.

Mark 4:36 *And when they had sent away the multitude, they took him even as he was in the ship. And there were also with him other little ships.*

After the multitude had been sent away "*they took him* [Jesus] *even as he was in the ship.*" They didn't go home to change clothes; they didn't run through the drive-thru for some sandwiches for the trip; they just pushed out from where they were. When we take Jesus "over there" we are to take Him just as He is. We are not to add anything to Him or take anything from Him. Jesus and His teachings are very plainly and thoroughly explained throughout the Bible; and anything that is added to or taken away from it are men's opinions and traditions. God blesses His Word and it alone. If your faith has stagnated, get back to the basics of the Word of God and move forward. When a church loses its objective of taking Jesus "over there" it must consider what all has been added to the plain teaching of the Word of God, and eliminate what has been added which has taken it off course.

"*And there were also with him other little ships.*" There are other believers as well as other churches "*with Him.*" While we can have fellowship with them, do not allow what they are doing or how God is leading them to side track you and keep you from the mission to take Jesus "over there."

Mark 4:37 *And there arose a great storm of wind, and the waves beat into the ship, so that it was now full.*

The men that were sailing the ship were for the most part fishermen who sailed the Sea of Galilee for a living. They were very used to the storms that arose on that body of water, and were probably not concerned at first. Everything was under control just as it had been in previous storms; so, they used all of their skills to keep the ship moving forward. Then the storm intensified into a "*great storm,*" and it became more than they could handle. The waves were not just beating *on* the ship, but were now beating *into* the ship. Waves beating onto the ship will give the sailors a wild ride, but it is not usually life threatening. Waves beating into the ship can sink the ship with all who are on board. To make things worse the ship "*was now full.*"

We expect problems, or storms, to come into our life and into the church. Normally we can handle them with the knowledge and skills God has given us in the past. However, when God is leading in a direction that we do not easily wish to follow, He needs to intensify the storms. He does this to get our attention and let us know beyond any doubt that it is Him that is moving in our life; and also, to demonstrate to us His power and strength in our lives to guide us safely through the storm while our faith grows and matures.

The men in the ship now have a choice to make. The ship appears to be sinking; and logic would have it that all were in great danger of losing their lives. They can either put on their life jackets, jump over board leaving the ship to the storm, and take their chances in the water; or they can wake up Jesus and see what He can do with this dire situation. Too often when the great storms come we tend to bail out from the place where Jesus has guided us to instead of "waking up" Jesus in our life. Too often we wrap ourselves in the life jackets of our addiction and comfort zone, and proclaiming that this "church thing" or this "Jesus thing" didn't work, we plunge ourselves into the storm somehow hoping to just survive. Jesus has allowed the storm into your life for a purpose. When we bail out and leave Him behind we are going backward instead of forward. When a church refuses to follow the explicit directions of Jesus as given in His Word, the church will no longer be on the mission of taking Jesus "over there."

Whenever the task is undertaken to take Jesus "over there" the question is never "if" there will be a storm but rather "when" there will be a storm. A person as well as a church cannot be actively engaged in the work of God without opposition from the enemy, Satan. He and his demons will work overtime through the thoughts of the unclean spirit in the minds of those involved to make sure they know all of the "reasons" why they should not be in this ship that is taking Jesus "over there.."

Notice that the storm in verse thirty-seven is a *"great storm of wind."* No one has ever seen the wind, but only the results of it as it blows trees and lawn furniture all over the place. The "wind" represents the spiritual work of the unclean spirit as it moves people in its wake. The waves beating into the ship are driven by the invisible wind; and those waves are representative of people who are opposing the work you are doing for Christ. People will give you many "reasons" why you cannot take Jesus "over there" in the church or in your life personally. People who allow the unclean spirit to affect their thoughts and actions will try to discourage you as you try to build your faith in Jesus. People under the direction of the unclean spirit will try to lure you back to your addiction; and just as the waves of the Sea of Galilee beat into the ship they will beat into your life.

If allowed to continue, the waves beating into the ship will have only one outcome, and that is to sink the ship. For the ship to survive this onslaught of water it must get away from the waves; but as it is tossed to and fro it is extremely difficult to control, especially when the waves are relentless and uncertain of when and what direction they are coming from. Many times, waves will be so powerful it is beyond the ability of the crew, regardless of how experienced they may be, to control the ship and save it from a watery end. When a person has been released from the control of the unclean spirit that has led to some addiction in their life they feel very much in control of things. It is only a matter of time before the "waves," which are the people driven and controlled by the unclean spirit, will begin to beat into their life and try to return them to the depths of their addiction.

Many times, these "waves" or people will be very good, longtime friends or even worse they may be relatives. The most persuasive people can be those you love or those who you look up to in life; but they can be controlled by the unclean spirit just as anyone else. The men on the ship had fished the waters of the Sea of Galilee most of their lives; and the waves that were now trying to sink them were familiar to them. However, just as they could not control the ship in the midst of the waves, neither can the person who is being buffeted and overwhelmed control those close to him who are encouraging him to return to his addiction. The only hope is to get away from that which is trying to break down your defenses and usually that is impossible on your own.

The ship was "*now full*." The men on the ship had a decision to make; and that decision needed to be made very quickly, or it would be too late. They could either grab anything that would float, and toss themselves into the very sea that was trying to consume them; or they could stay the course where Jesus was and had taken them. As the temptations from the unclean spirit overwhelm the now freed addict to return, the same decision must be made. He can either grab what he thinks will keep him "afloat," which is his former addiction, and plunge himself back into the culture and people that were trying to destroy him; or he can stay in the place where Jesus has him, and rely on Jesus to continue to direct in his life.

Mark 4:38 *And he [Jesus] was in the hinder part of the ship, asleep on a pillow: and they awake him, and say unto him, Master, carest thou not that we perish?*

Where was Jesus? Had He left the men and abandoned them? Had the storm even bothered Him? Absolutely not! We see Jesus very calmly asleep in the hinder, or rear, part of the ship on a pillow. The storm was not even a consideration to Him because He had total control over it. Things we can control in life do not seem to concern us; but the things we cannot control will drive us to make bad choices. Many times, we try to mask the uncontrolled thing in our life with a temporary relief from it instead of dealing with the source of the issue. The old saying, "Don't put off until tomorrow what you can do today," rings true. When we "put off" dealing with the issues in our life such as the hurt feelings; the out of control situations; and the guilt or loneliness often felt, the unclean spirit will bring thoughts into our mind that "this will make you feel better," or "this will make it go away." However, the issue is still there and is growing until it is addressed at its root. Jesus was in the "*hinder part of the ship*" out of sight of the crew. Just because we cannot "see" Jesus in our life does not mean He is not there with us.

The men made the right choice, but went about it in a poor manner. They didn't jump overboard and abandon what Jesus had given them for a mission, to take Jesus over there, but stayed in the ship with Jesus. The men *"awake him"* from His sleep. As the waves beat into our life we need to "wake up" Jesus in our life. It isn't that He has gone to sleep, but that we have allowed Him and His direction to take a back seat to our will. When we "wake up Jesus" in our life we turn to Him for guidance, and abandon any sense of control we think we have over the situation. We too can get into a situation where we don't think He cares for us. Many men and women that come into the jail come with the attitude that Jesus doesn't care about them because of what they did. When Jesus draws near to them with His great love through the chapel services, the Bible study lessons, and the Christian books, they see that they are in that place so Jesus can draw them closer to Himself. They "wake up" Jesus in their life.

The work of the unclean spirit has no bounds in a person's life if it is allowed to remain and be considered. We saw in chapter one the total control the unclean spirit had over the man from the tombs in Gadara. Now, the unclean spirit has stirred up the crew of the ship to the point they were convinced they would perish. They were so given over to the influence of the unclean spirit that they forgot the words of Jesus when they began their journey, *"Let us pass over unto the other side."* The key word in that statement is the word "us." With Jesus onboard, they would not perish. Had they abandoned Jesus their fate would have been sealed in the waves. When a person loses sight of the direction and purpose Jesus has for them, and returns to the "old ways" they begin to accuse God of not caring; but He does and always will regardless of the things of the past.

Mark 4:39 *And he arose, and rebuked the wind, and said unto the sea, Peace, be still. And the wind ceased, and there was a great calm.*

As soon as the crew of the ship realized they could no longer control the situation and turned to Jesus He *"arose, and rebuked the wind."* Jesus went right to work and went right to the source of the entire situation, the wind. Had the wind not been driving the waves there would have been no situation. When Jesus rebuked the wind, He demonstrated His absolute control over nature. To the north of the Sea of Galilee is Mt. Hermon which at times may have snow upon it. The temperature difference and the atmospheric difference between the top of Mt. Hermon and the Sea of Galilee can be great at times. The terrain between Mt. Hermon and the Sea of Galilee is filled with canyons and valleys which act as funnels for the wind created by the differences in the atmospheres. When Jesus rebuked the wind, He addressed the root of the wind which was the atmospheric differences between the two locations; and the wind ceased. This was something totally impossible with the men in the ship. Luke 18:27 *"And he said, The things which are impossible with men are possible with God."*

Then Jesus addressed the waves and simply said to them, *"Peace, be still."* If that would be a scene from something Hollywood produced, they would have some burly actor standing on the side of the ship waving his arms and screaming at the waves. That is man's version. Jesus simply "said" to the waves in a voice that was not raised, or anything above His normal voice, *"Peace, be still."* When Jesus takes over our situation He simply addresses the "waves," which are those who are trying to influence us to consider the prompting of the unclean spirit, and stills them in our life.

"And the wind ceased, and there was a great calm." Now there is a different problem presented in the journey to take Jesus "over there." There is no wind. When the men began their journey to take Jesus "over there," they pushed the ship away from the shore, hoisted up the sails, and away they went. Now they are not at their destination, and the thing that was propelling them, the wind, was no longer available. To reach their destination they must now work. Every man was needed to pick up the oars and start rowing.

Far too many people return to their addiction because they fail to realize they must "work" at keeping the unclean spirit from returning to control. They cannot sit around with the same old friends and allow themselves to be caught up in the same environment as before if they want to stay addiction-free. New friends must be established who are Christians, and will engage in encouraging them to stay on the right path. Establishing an entirely new lifestyle takes planning and work, and must be done in obedience to the leadership of the Holy Spirit. Once the "waves" have been stilled and the "wind" has been rebuked, too many people simply want to sit in the "great calm" waiting for God to do something, when it is up to them to "work" to get to their appointed destination.

For the church's part every person in the church must be involved in the mission of taking Jesus "over there." That includes getting involved with presenting the love and acceptance Jesus has for the one who is trying to establish new things in their life, and centering those things around Jesus. When the great calm came upon the Sea of Galilee, everyone on the ship was exceedingly relieved that the danger had passed and they were safe. When problems within a church are resolved and the "waves" that were beating into it have been stilled, everyone rejoices and breathes a sigh of relief. That can be a very dangerous time also if the church does not immediately resume the task given them, and continue to take Jesus "over there." When complacency sets into a church the one who is seeking encouragement and Christian fellowship in their life will not find it. That can discourage the one seeking and allows them to slip back into the same old things and ways; and the control of the unclean spirit returns.

As the crew of the ship realized they still needed to move onward in their journey, they picked up their assigned oars and they all began to row. What would happen if all of the men on the left side of the ship decided they were hungry, and very tired from the battle with the storm, and left their oars for something to eat and a nap? The ship would go around in circles and never reach their destination. Jesus and His saving message would be stuck going in circles in the middle of nowhere. Or what if every other man decided to take a nap for a time and let the remaining men pull all of the load? Those doing all of the work would not get the ship to their destination in a timely manner; and before too long they would tire and stop. Either way, those who were to be the recipients of taking Jesus "over there" would not hear because they were at the place where Jesus was supposed to be, but the message of Jesus was not. Thus, the mission would be a failure. It takes every person, regardless of age, physical condition, or busy schedules to pull on the oars to get Jesus "over there" when He needs to be "over there." When only a few people do all of the work the mission will not be as planned by Jesus; and more failures will be realized than successes. The failure of all of the church members to participate to their fullest is a very large reason why people return to their addictions and allow the unclean spirit to resume control of their life.

Mark 4:40 *And he said unto them, Why are ye so fearful? how is it that ye have no faith?*

Faith and fear are complete opposites of each other. If we have faith we have no fear; and if we have fear, it is because we have no faith. The church's mission is to take Jesus "over there;" and when this is done in faith the wind and the waves that beat into it are all handled in Jesus' power, and can be seen as mere distractions along the journey. When Jesus is in the church just as He was in the ship, He questions why we become so fearful when things don't go the way we think they should go. When the church members insist upon doing things their way instead of the way God is leading them simply because "this is how we always have done it," the mission will not be accomplished for God's glory.

Storms of life will translate to storms within the church, and every one of them have a planned purpose in the will of God. Too often we as church members look at the storms, try to analyze them, and try to stop them before God has decreed; thus, the purpose of the storm is not accomplished. Storms in life as well as in the church build faith by strengthening and maturing what little faith already exists. The men on the ship needed their faith to be challenged so they would realize Jesus

64

is totally in charge. The storm got them asking questions and thinking about who Jesus really was, and what all He can do.

Mark 4:41 *"And they feared exceedingly, and said one to another, What manner of man is this, that even the wind and the sea obey him?"*

They saw Him as a "man" but the storm revealed Him as God. The purpose for storms in our lives is to get us to look to Jesus not only for deliverance, but for our faith to grow in Him.

I hear regularly from inmates that I minister to how the "great storm" that they are in, which brought them to the place of incarceration has opened their spiritual eyes to what it is that Jesus is trying to do in their lives. Many still do not realize what truly is happening in their lives, and still believe themselves to be "alright." In God's timing He will deal more strongly with them, but the time is not yet. For those who realize the purpose of the storm, it is a marvellous privilege that God has given me, as well as our volunteers, to help them sort out the plan God has for them, as it has been so clearly revealed in the Bible. Questions are being asked and considered about this One called Jesus who wants to love them and control their life for God's glory and for their blessing. While they are incarcerated within the jail, I can provide them with as much knowledge as God allows me to share with them, as well as bring others in to help teach them through our Bible studies and chapel services. We can be a part of the beginning of a great work in their lives, but that is all we can do.

Most men and women who are incarcerated in our county jail are released or ordered to another facility for instruction concerning their addictions. Through the Prison Discipleship Ministry, we are able to stay with them and follow them with the Bible study lessons they are working on while with us. What they need is to be shown the next step in their newly found faith, and that is active involvement in a local church with other believers who will continue what has been started in their lives. Through the follow-up program of the Prison Discipleship Ministry we can refer these precious souls to a local Bible teaching, Bible believing church; but then it is up to the church to step forward and make them feel very welcomed, as well as shown the love Christ has for them. If the church has been side-tracked by a "storm" and every person is not "manning the oars" the church will fail in their mission. The once addicted person will go away wondering what the church is really all about, and the chances are very great that they will return to the control of the unclean spirit.

The title of this chapter is "Why a Storm?" The purpose for the storms is made so very clear in the verses we have been considering in Mark chapters four and five. Jesus gave the command for them to *"pass over unto the other side"* in Mark 4:35. Did you notice that it is not recorded exactly where He said to go? He simply wanted them to push off and begin the journey much like He wants us to do in faith. As the ship was underway it was going in a direction that the helmsman was guiding it towards and would have reached somewhere on the other side had they continued on that course. Jesus, knowing the exact purpose of the journey, went to sleep to rest since He was still very much human and exhausted, and allowed the storm to overtake the ship. It was tossed here and there, forward and backward, rolling side to side, and the helmsman had little to no control of the direction the ship was now going. When the storm was stilled by Jesus the ship was pointed in the right direction that Jesus wanted; and all that was needed was the work of the crew to row it to its destination.

Mark 5:2 *"And when he [Jesus] was come out of the ship, immediately there met him out of the tombs a man with an unclean spirit."*

Notice the word "immediately." Jesus had used the storm to put the ship on the exact course to meet this man within the exact six-foot piece of coastline where he was at, and at the exact time that he was there. The purpose Jesus had for passing over unto the other side was to meet this one man who had a great need in his life for Jesus. Had the crew been allowed to steer the ship they would have landed somewhere, but not where this man was at the exact time he was there. There would have been others that possibly would

66

have heard the message Jesus had, but the object of Jesus' great love at that moment was that one precious soul who would go on to witness for Jesus and open the door for Jesus to do even more work (see chapter one).

Storms in life and storms within the church will come, but they do not need to be feared. While they are unpleasant to pass through they have a purpose in God's plan that is much greater than our short period of rebellious comfort and pleasure. When the storms that come are viewed with the faith that Jesus is in total control, and has allowed this to happen for a purpose, the storm will take on new meaning.

Jeremiah 33:3 Call *unto me, and I will answer thee, and shew thee great and mighty things, which thou knowest not.*

Simply follow Jesus!

"I pray to God I never come back to this place." That was my prayer on the day that I met the One who sailed up to the shore below the tombs where I was living. He stepped out of the ship and onto the land; and from the moment I laid my eyes upon Him my life has never been the same. As I ran down the hill towards Him I felt a burning and a longing within my heart that I never felt before. Many had come to that shore, with chains and fetters to bind me and change me but none like Him. As I knelt at His feet I experienced a peace within my mind and heart beyond words, and my entire life took on meaning and purpose; but I have gotten ahead of what I wish to tell you.

Please allow me to introduce myself. Even though my name is not recorded in the Bible, I do have a name. It is a name most people in your part of the world cannot pronounce or even spell so you can just call me James. Even though there are many different people named James recorded in the Bible, I am not one of them. I am thirty-eight years old, and have lived in the vicinity of Gadara all of my life. I have family and relatives living throughout the region of Decapolis, and I know the country very well. I was employed at a trade which I enjoyed very much, and I don't mind telling you, was very good at. My lovely wife has given me four amazing children whom I love with all of my heart. The littlest one is the most creative little boy you have ever seen. He can find more ways to get into trouble than anyone can imagine, but how he does it is always in a unique way. One day he will grow up to be a natural leader of men. He is so very compassionate to the other children, and is demonstrating a kindness that will surely help others who are in great need in the future. The other three have different talents that are developing, and it is a joyous time to watch how they are growing physically as well as emotionally.

My beautiful wife is the love of my life. We met and married when we were very young; and through the years together she has been my trusted best friend and companion for life. The love we have for each other grows as the years pass. Besides that, she is the greatest cook one could ever know. This extra "spare tire" around my waist didn't just happen. Her fabulous cooking is directly responsible for it, and I enjoy letting her know that. One might look at my life and be very jealous with all of the blessings I have been given.

As I mentioned, I have a job that I thoroughly enjoy. I think the best part is the guys I work with. They are a little rough around the edges, and most of them don't seem to have the good family life that I have. They spend a lot of time after work together going places and visiting places that I don't particularly care for, but they always seem to have fun. They kept inviting me to go with them on the weekends, and I kept telling them I have all that I need at home. They can be very persuasive so one day I decided to go with them just to get them off my back. Looking back now, that was probably one of the stupidest choices I ever made.

My wife was not really happy that I was not going to be at home with her and the kids, but I reasoned within myself that I needed a little "me time" once in a while. Me and the guys started out at one of their houses and then went from place to place. They gave me things to eat and drink that I never tasted before. Some tasted okay, but some of it was absolutely awful. However, I endured for the sake of not wanting to look foolish in front of the guys. As the day dragged on I started feeling very different, unlike I ever felt before. I wasn't sure if I liked it, but we seemed to be having a good time. At least that's what everyone was telling me. By the time I finally arrived home it was really difficult to think clearly, and all I wanted to do was get some sleep. My wife was visibly upset and wanted to know if I was still going to take the kids to the park like I had promised earlier that week. I don't remember what I said to her before I fell asleep, but she became very quiet.

The silent treatment continued the next morning and breakfast wasn't the usual sumptuous feast. She was not happy with me and was letting me know it in her own way. She asked me if I was going to go with the guys anymore or not, and I replied rather harshly that I might. Where did that come from? I never spoke to my sweet wife in that tone of voice before. Even when we didn't agree on something there was always a bond of love that kept us both on the same page of the conversation. Now this attitude out of my mouth. I hated myself for it, but didn't do anything about it. There was no goodbye kiss when I left for work, and the walk to work was just awful. All throughout the day the guys at work talked about all the "fun" we had during our time together and how much they were looking forward to doing it again. That was the last thing I wanted to do; but I didn't want to seem like a whimp in their eyes, so I half-heartedly agreed.

Over the next few weeks I found myself with them more than with my family. The things they were giving me began to taste good, and I began to look forward to them. My attitude towards my wife and kids continued to change; and while I still loved them very much, I had an extremely hard time expressing it properly. Home life began to be difficult, and I did not look forward to going home after work to the harsh words from my wife and kids who didn't seem to understand my feelings anymore. As the months passed it became very apparent that my time at home was coming to an end. One of the guys at work who was single told me I could crash at his place if things got too rough at my house, and that is what I did. I knew I should have swallowed my pride and gone back home to work things out, but that became something I really did not want to do. She had no right telling me how to run my life, and she needed to know I was serious about having my own space.

Living at my friend's house was one party after another; and the things we were doing began to take on a new meaning in my life. It seemed as if my life was being defined by them; and the things I had valued so dearly before were just faint memories. I spent time moving from place to place over the next year. It seemed as if my welcome was soon worn out at one place, and I would move in with someone else. I tried to visit my wife and kids, but they shunned me and even told me I was not welcomed at home anymore. They were very emphatic about their dislike for the person I had become. My wife kept nagging me to stop and get help, and it seemed like I could not convince her that I had everything under control. I knew I was lying to her, but I had to keep up my image.

Having things under control was the last thing that was going on in my life at that point. My thoughts were constantly on the next good time with the guys. Even my boss didn't seem to understand me anymore. He was a guy with a family just like me, and he liked to have fun just like me; so why didn't he understand when my work slacked off, and I began to come in late a few times? One day he called me into his office and told me that I was no longer a benefit to the company, and he was letting me go. Fired! That had never happened in my entire life. Doesn't he know how good I am at my job? All I could think of was how little he appreciated me after all of the years I had given him. I was angry with him when I stormed out of the office door, but it seemed as if I was now free to enjoy myself and indulge myself even more. The thought of no income to pay for the habits I had never entered my mind. I knew the guys would understand and help me through this tough time.

That didn't work out too well, and very quickly I found myself without any friends or any place to stay. I remembered meeting a guy at one of the parties that told me about some caves up in the hills overlooking the Sea of Galilee where people lived who didn't have any place to go. He said it was great up there because nobody bothered them or cared what you did. I headed up there only to find out that the caves were actually tombs. Tombs! Tombs are full of the bones of dead people! I remember thinking how cool that was, which was an indication of how far my thought process had been affected by the things I had chosen to control me. The tombs were a place filled with men and women living there who were thieves and murderers, as well as those who were doing the same things as I was. There was no law within the tombs, and everyone did what they pleased. It was a terrifying place, and I had to be on my guard every moment. It was survival of the strongest, and everyone had their own territory they tried to protect with whatever amount of violence was needed.

I was trapped with absolutely no hope for the future. How ironic it was that the very things I was allowing into my life would one day kill me while living in the place of the dead already, the tombs. There were times when things seemed to clear up in my mind, and I would hate who I had become; especially when thoughts of my wife and kids would come to mind. I found myself crying most nights, and running wildly throughout the mountains surrounding the tombs looking for that one way to escape this terrible nightmare I was living. The thing that I had allowed into my life for a moment of pleasure was now well into the process of destroying me with no hope in sight. I began to cut myself with stones (Mark 5:5) out of desperation to end it all. My reasoning was that surely death would be better than what I was going through. However, day after day, night after endless night there was no hope to be found.

Men from the city and the surrounding villages would grab me and put chains around me; but this thing that was controlling me had given me unhuman strength, and I was able to break the chains at will and flee (Mark 5:4). The others in the tombs stayed away from me because they knew my strength was no match for any of them, and my anger would turn that strength upon them at the slightest provocation. Time passed and became a blur in my mind. Less and less were the thoughts of my family and the wonderful life I had before this thing took over. Death would be a welcomed thing, but I lacked the courage to pursue it seriously. Later, I would see what a blessing that "weakness" would prove to be.

Then one day a fishing ship landed on the shore below the tombs. That was unusual since there were many fishing ships that fished the waters off the coast, but no one ever actually landed in that particular area unless they were after me with those chains. The reputation of us who lived in the tombs was widely known, and no one wanted to have anything to do with us for fear of their lives. However, this ship landed directly below where I was sitting, and to my absolute amazement a man stepped out onto the shore. Who was this guy? Was he a stranger to the area and didn't know who we were up here? Didn't he realize he was in great danger of being robbed and even killed just for the clothes he wore? I sat for a few minutes and watched him. He was different than anyone I had ever seen, but I could not explain why. At last, I reasoned, this might be the one who could help me rid myself of the thing that was controlling me. I stood up and ran towards him. Something inside of me was telling me that this was the One who knew everything I needed, and as I began my run towards Him I think I noticed a glimmer of a smile on His face while the others with Him looked absolutely terrified. I fell at His feet, and I opened my heart to Him (Mark 5:6). I found worshipping Him was easy and very pleasant.

Many had tried to help me with this thing that controlled me, but they all spoke to me as an outcast, as someone they would rather not be talking with but out of some misplaced sense of duty felt it necessary. This Man was different. His words were gentle and yet strong. He didn't speak to me, but directed His command to that thing inside of me that had me so controlled. He said, "Come out of the man thou unclean spirit" (Mark 5:8). As He spoke it seemed He was having a conversation with someone else, but He was looking directly at me. Then He asked "What is thy name?" (Mark 5:9). As I started to answer Him I found that I could not speak. This Man who I found out later was named Jesus was addressing the very thing that was controlling me, and identified it as an "unclean spirit" (Mark 5:8). The only voice I heard was His and then He gave a nod as if to grant a request (Mark 5:13). Immediately, the herd of pigs that were grazing behind me and up the hill began to squeal and run violently down the hill, over the edge of the cliff, and into the sea. I saw them no more.

Something was very different. Something within me had changed, and I was not sure exactly what it was. I felt very calm and for the first time in a long time I was able to process thoughts. I discovered that I was almost naked and felt very embarrassed. Someone from the ship that was with Jesus gave me his coat to put on, and I felt very comfortable. I looked at the cuts on my arms, and was repulsed by the scars that were so prominent from all of the many times I had cut myself severely attempting to escape the control of what I now realized was an unclean spirit.

The men that tended to the pigs ran into town and told the owners of the herd what had happened not only to his animals, but to me also (Mark 5:14). As people from town began to gather around they spoke mean words to Jesus, and accused Him of destroying their property. They told Him and those with Him not to stay, but to board the ship and sail out of that place. There was a look of fear mixed with anger on their faces (Mark 5:15-17). I stayed near to Jesus for as long as I could. When I saw He was leaving I begged Him to allow me to come with Him in the ship and stay with Him (Mark 5:18). I did not want what I was feeling to ever end, and I certainly did not want to go back to where I came from. I had no ties to that horrible place that I called home for so long, and desired even the memory of it to fade away. I could be of some service to Jesus if I were allowed to stay with Him because I knew how to repair many things, and I wasn't too bad of a cook either. Surely, He would have a need for me. Don't allow me to go back to the tombs where I came from! I pray to God that I never return to that place again.

As Jesus stepped into the ship I was prepared to step in after Him, but He turned and spoke to me personally and not to that awful unclean spirit that was now gone. His eyes were so kind and yet so very firm as He addressed me and said, "Go home to thy friends, and tell them how great things the Lord hath done for thee, and hath had compassion on thee" (Mark 5:19). Go home! The sound of those words flashed thoughts into my mind that I had not had in a very long time. They were thoughts of my home with my dear loving wife, my children, and even a brief thought of the cat that keeps the occasional mouse out. All I could think about was my family and my friends that I had abandoned for the sake of a little pleasure and a lot of misery. Could it be possible that I could return home again? Would my wife and children still be there, and if they were would they want to have anything to do with me? Fear mingled with anticipation gripped me, and all I could do was stand there and watch as Jesus stepped into the ship and sailed away with those men that came with Him.

Chapter 9 The Journey Back

I stood on the shore and watched until the ship carrying Jesus and His men was out of sight. Thoughts were racing through my mind so fast I didn't know what to do next, so I just sat down to think. I could scarcely believe what had just happened to me. The unclean spirit that had come to me so long ago and took control of my life was gone. I had begged Jesus to take me with Him, but He told me to go back home and tell my family and friends what had happened. He wanted me to tell them of His great compassion that was shown to me (Mark 5:19). He had every right to try to bind me as all of the others had done, or even worse He could have ignored me. Instead, in His marvellous love for me He delivered me from the control of the unclean spirit. Not only was I set free but I was given an assignment from Him to tell others. I had only seen Jesus for a very short time and now He was gone, but in my heart, I felt as if He were still with me.

As the day wore on I realized that the last thing I could do was to sit on the shore by myself. I had to do something, but what? One thing was absolutely certain. I could never return to those awful tombs and the people who dwelt in them. There was nothing for me there anymore, and I needed to move on with my life. I must do as Jesus said and go back home. It would be dark soon, and the hill country was not a safe place to be alone at night. It was only a few miles back to my home, and the sooner I started the sooner I would be among the safety of my family and friends.

The road was particularly dusty since there had been no rain in several weeks, and the hot summer sun had dried everything out as it normally does this time of year. As I walked I began to think about my wife and children, but particularly about my wife. How will I ever be accepted back into her home, and more importantly back into her heart? I had been neglectful to her, and one might say even abusive as I made my choices. What I put her through should never be placed upon anyone, especially one that is so very much loved. Her eyes are what attracted me to her when we first met. They were brilliantly brown and had a playfulness about them that I could not resist. She did not need to speak a word, and I knew by looking into her eyes what she was thinking. What a treasure I was given in her love for me. Then to see those beautiful eyes filled with tears of hurt and betrayal was almost too much to think about. As I became more selfishly involved in the things of my pleasure, those tender, playful eyes began to grow cold. I could almost see what appeared to be a hatred in them instead of the love that once radiated so abundantly from them. How could I ever return to her? How could I ever expect her to understand my deep sorrow for the things that I did to hurt her? How could I ever expect her to forgive me for abandoning her with the children for such a long time? What if she doesn't want me back?

The thought of losing her was unbearable, but the thought of facing her and seeing once again the results of what I had done was even more unbearable. I cannot return home. Not after all I have done. How could Jesus tell me to return to her? Maybe I will just sleep somewhere in the city, and casually see her from time to time. Maybe if given enough time she will begin to have good feelings towards me again. The thoughts kept coming, and as I kept walking I didn't know what to do. Jesus had clearly given me a direction and an assignment, but how could He know what she would be like if I just showed up? The thoughts of terror began to overwhelm me, and it seemed like they were wanting to control me once again and get me to doubt what Jesus had said was the truth. I must not listen to these thoughts. I must do exactly what Jesus told me to do. Wasn't He the only One out of many to set me free from that unclean spirit and its influence and control in my life? Hadn't others tried to tame me with my radically violent actions and all had failed (Mark 5:4)? Why should I listen to another unclean spirit that is trying to get me to do exactly what I did to get into all of the trouble in the first place? Why should I even think I could go against Jesus' words of truth?

The battle in my mind went on for what seemed like hours. When I thought I had made up my mind to follow what Jesus had told me to do, the unclean spirit would pop another doubt into my mind and it would sound logical to me. When I would consider the unclean spirit's thoughts I began to be fearful of the outcome; but when I would firmly stand on what Jesus had told me to do a peace came over me like at the first. I resolved to follow Jesus' words and go directly back to my wife. That became a settled issue, and I would face whatever consequences awaited me with her. No sooner than that was settled the thoughts of my kids began to flood my mind. How could they ever be expected to have anything to do with a Dad that was a total embarrassment to them in school and with their friends? They were the kids of that crazy guy living in the tombs, and I am certain they heard that every day while I was gone. How could they forgive me for such an embarrassment? How could they ever trust me again after I left them? The moment they start trusting that I would be there for them I might disappear again or even worse, they might hear that I died. I would be like a stranger to them even though I still loved them more than life itself. The special creativeness of my little one, the talents of the oldest boy, the silly fun of the girls, and the scene they showed forth when they were all together playing and laughing and enjoying life. How could I ever be a part of that once again? My wife might learn to accept me back into her life in time, but the hurt I have caused those precious young ones may last for the rest of their lives. How could I ever endure that in my life? Jesus is asking too much of me, and I don't want to cause my family even more hurt than I have already caused. The fear returned again four-fold, one for each child.

However, what is the alternative? Returning to the tombs, the people I was with, and the lifestyle I was living was not even an option. It now was repulsive to me, and the only option is to follow Jesus' instructions and go back home. I had caused the hurt, and I must face the consequences regardless of how severe they would be. After all, didn't Jesus direct me on this path? He alone was the One that spoke truth and set me free, so why would His instructions be feared? The fearful thoughts are certainly not coming from Jesus, but from the one that wants to control me again and pull me away from Jesus.

As I reached the top of the last hill I saw the lights flickering from the window in my house. It was almost supper time, and soon the smell of something wonderful cooking would fill the air. The children would be helping with the meal, all except the little one who would be trying to see how firmly attached the cat's tail was to it. I paused to consider what the next few moments would bring and how much I loved each of them, but especially my wife. I missed her more than I realized, and now the feelings of warmth and love flooded over my mind and heart to the point of almost being overwhelming. There was a part of me that wanted to break out in a run, and burst through the door hugging and kissing as I made my way through the room. Another part of me began to entertain the fear that gripped me on the road. It was still not too late to turn around and leave, and not face the disappointment that may be waiting inside that cozy home. One thing I learned that day was the unclean spirit never ever gives up. It may be quiet for a brief period of time, but it will always try to enter into my thoughts over and over again. It was an effort to make my feet move down the last little incline to the pathway that leads to the front door. It wasn't actually a door this time of year, but only a cloth hanging in the doorway to help keep the bugs out and give a small degree of privacy.

As I approached the doorway I very softly called out my wife's name. There was no response from inside. I called again a little louder. Suddenly all of the sounds that had been coming from inside stopped, and there was total silence. After what seemed like an eternity the cloth door covering moved to the side slightly, and I could see my wife looking out at me with a look of fear in her beautiful brown eyes. This was the moment I had so greatly anticipated and feared all at the same time. I wanted to reach out to her and embrace her, but at the same time I wanted to run as fast as I could. The curtain parted to the side more and revealed her standing there with the look of fear still on her face. I spoke her name once again softly, and she came through the doorway and put her arms around my neck, kissing my cheek with tears of joy in her eyes and a smile on her face. The sound of my voice speaking her name was all she needed to know I was not the same man that left her, and caused her all of the hurt for so very long. As I held her I glanced over her shoulder and peeking out of the doorway were four sets of eyes not knowing what to make of the situation. A look of uncertainty mixed with curiosity filled their faces. With the assurance that all was well from their Mom they came out of the door and hugged my legs as only children can do.

The fear that had gripped me concerning my welcome or rejection by my family was gone completely. As I thought about it, I was so very thankful that I had not chosen to listen to the voice of the unclean spirit and run. What made the difference with my wife and children? When I saw them the last time there were angry words and a tension filled the air so thick it could almost be cut with a knife. Now, to be welcomed back so graciously and lovingly after so much hurt was beyond comprehension. As my wife and I talked well into the night, having tucked the kids into bed with hugs and kisses, I discovered there was not a day or night that my wife and children had not prayed for God to bring me back to them, but not as I was. They prayed for God to do a great work in my life, and restore me back to what God had intended me to be all along, a loving husband and Dad. All of the time I was allowing the unclean spirit to control my life, I was unaware that my family was seeking God's intervention in bringing me back to them.

What amazed me more than anything was the thoughts that had once been running through my mind the entire time I was in the tombs and running out of control. Thoughts of how my family didn't love me, and how they would never take me back. Thoughts of other people hating me, and wanting to bind me with chains and even kill me. Those thoughts had kept coming at a pace that was beyond imagination. The more they kept pounding me with their hateful and vicious suggestions the more my life projected those feelings upon myself and others. Over the next few days I had time to spend with my family in an atmosphere of love and tenderness, and I had time to reflect on where I went wrong. I realized that everything began to disintegrate when that first thought was placed in my mind from the unclean spirit telling me that I needed some "me time" and I could find pleasure in the company of the guys rather than in the family that loved me. I had allowed the thoughts that I knew were wrong to remain in my mind and to grow rather than reject them for what I knew to be the truth. How could I have ever been so blind and so careless with what I allowed into my mind? One thing was certain, I will never allow that to happen again.

As the days passed I remembered the words of Jesus as He was getting into the ship just before He sailed away. "Go home to thy friends, and tell them how great things the Lord hath done for thee, and hath had compassion on thee." (Mark 5:19) I had been given an assignment that I must fulfill. I must begin to tell others about this One named Jesus that I had met while I was at the bottom of my life, and how He restored me.

But where do I start? The instructions from Jesus did not mention any particular area or any particular people so I didn't know how to begin. As I was thinking on these things I heard a familiar voice outside of my door calling my name. The man I had worked for and who had fired me was standing right outside my door wanting to speak with me. A moment of fear gripped my entire body and I froze. Should I answer him or let him think I was not home? What if he wanted to tell me how much I had hurt the company and how production had dropped? What if he wanted some kind of revenge? He is a big man and could put the hurts on a person if he decided to. I went to the door and partially drew the curtain back. Standing there with a huge smile on his face was this very large man speaking my name in a tone that I knew was not aimed to hurt me.

I invited him in and as we talked he told me that he would like me to return since I was one of the best employees he ever had. I told him how things had developed between me and the guys that worked there, and that I would not be comfortable working with them again. Then he told me about a new position he wanted to create, and that he thought I would be the perfect man for the job. He wanted to expand the market for his products and was wanting to hire me as an outside salesman. The pay he offered was great, but it would involve some travel throughout the region. I asked him to let me think about it over that night and, of course, talk with my wife about it before letting him know in the morning.

My wife and I talked it over throughout the evening, and discussed all of the advantages, as well as the disadvantages. It seemed she was in favor of me accepting his offer, but did not cherish the thought of me being gone from home. We did need the income since we had dug a very deep hole financially while I was away from them. Sleep was hard that night because I kept thinking about everything connected with the job proposal. What if the people I called upon in my new position knew who I was, what I had done, and rejected me? What if they spread gossip throughout the region so that my family was shamed, and I would not be able to find work? How could someone like me with the past reputation I had ever be trusted to be away from home and on my own without going back to where I came from? As I laid there I remembered the words of Jesus and the assignment He had given me. Then the thought came clearly that this is how Jesus wanted me to carry out my assignment. This was an opportunity He had given me to tell others about what He had done for me. Instead of hiding my past from them, I would use the deliverance Jesus had given me to tell others of His amazing love and compassion He has for them, if they will only trust Him. What had been a night of fear and thoughts of defeat was now clearly seen as the unclean spirit's attempt to keep me from following Jesus as He opened the way for me to serve Him.

As the boss and I talked in his office the next morning he was overjoyed with my decision to accept his offer. He told me they had developed some new products and had improved on some of the existing ones. I would need to spend some time in the shop updating my knowledge before I ventured out to sell. I agreed, but immediately upon hearing that my stomach tightened in a knot with fear. I would be working around the same guys I had been with before. How would they treat me? What would they say to me for going off of the deep end? How genuine would they see my attitude now? Would they taunt me into joining them once again in their sinful ventures? Maybe this whole thing was a big mistake, and I should never have accepted the job in the first place. There was no time or opportunity to run at this point since the boss got up and took me directly to the shop and into the presence of the guys. To my utter surprise they greeted me with a warmth and kindness that reassured me they were glad to see I was back, and was away from the horrible things I had allowed to control me. What a relief. Why had I allowed the thoughts of rejection and the fear that gripped me to even be a part of my thoughts? Jesus had given me an assignment and He would work out all of the details if I just trusted Him.

The few weeks in the shop went well, but I was still very cautious around the guys. They still liked to venture into sinful things, but it seemed they listened to me more intently as the days passed about what Jesus had done for me. We would talk awhile, and then they would change the subject trying to get me to give in to their ways and rejoin them in their "fun." I found an inner strength within me to reject their luring that could only come from God. As long as I kept the assignment that Jesus gave me to tell others what He did for me that day on the shore in my mind I could stay focused; but if I allowed their conversation to be considered in my thoughts I would stray from what my purpose was. I needed to learn more about God and this One named Jesus. I needed to find someone who knew the truth and was willing to teach me.

After several weeks spent in the shop I was on my way home, and was thinking about my desire to learn more about God so I wouldn't have such a difficult time with negative thoughts trying to pull me back where I had been. However, the only people I knew never talked about God or Jesus. It was as if they had never heard of either one of them. I arrived home and was greeted by the usual kiss from my wife, and hugs and kisses from the kids. It was so very good to be home instead of in those dreadful, wicked tombs. Just before supper was finished my wife casually mentioned that her Mom and Dad would be coming to visit in two days, and wanted to spend some time with the grandkids. It seemed like my entire world came crashing down with that news. I liked my in-laws, but I had not seen or heard from them since I went off on my own and treated my wife, their only daughter, so terribly. What would they say to me? How would they treat me? How should I act in their presence? Maybe I could talk the boss into letting me start my first road trip a few days early. After all, work is work. My mind was once again whirling with thoughts of what might happen, all negative of course. Why do I let these things consume my thoughts? What is the purpose, if any, behind them? Why can't I stop them? All I could think of was the pending and fast approaching encounter with my in-laws, and the embarrassment it could bring. My wife saw how upset I was and all she would say was that it would be alright, and everything would work out. I know she was trying to encourage me and calm me down, but it was not her that had to face them after what I had done. I wished I knew how to control all of the feelings of fear that kept coming.

The day finally came when my wife's parents would be at the house when I got home from work. The walk that I usually enjoyed as I looked forward to being with my family seemed to be a drudgery. Every possible thing that could go wrong kept playing out in my mind. I realized that running was not an option, but the thought of it was there all the way home. As I stood on the little hill above my home I could see a donkey grazing next to the house, and I knew they had arrived. My stomach knotted up and my steps slowed, but I made it to the doorway and forced myself to go in. To my surprise there were smiles and hugs that greeted me instead of anger and criticism. The knots in my stomach disappeared as we sat and enjoyed each other's company. My wife had prepared the best meal ever, and the kids were a delight around their grandparents who they had not seen in a long time. The little one was his usual self, getting laughs from everyone with his antics. As we sat and ate I told them about my new position at the company in outside sales, and I would be traveling some throughout the region of Decapolis introducing our products to new customers. My father-in-law invited me to stay at their house which was in the center of the southern area I would be travelling in. I thanked him and could not help but think how God was working out all of the details for me to carry out the assignment Jesus had given me.

Through the next several days my father-in-law and I talked, and his gentle way with me put me at ease about speaking of the things of the past. As I spoke to him about Jesus and what this Man had done for me in ridding me of the control of the unclean spirit, he listened intently. I told him I would like to learn more about God, and especially about this One named Jesus. He agreed and told me that he had heard vague things about Him, but had never met anyone who had actually seen Him. He and his friends were not sure if Jesus was a real person or just something someone made up. Now that he knew I had actually seen Him, and was delivered from the control of the unclean spirit within me, he also wanted to know more. As we talked some of our neighbors gathered for a leisurely evening together, and the talk centered around this One named Jesus.

As I shared what He had done for me I discovered they were all curious, but had been fearful to mention their desire to know more not wanting anyone to think they were chasing a myth if it were not true. Knowing I had actually met Jesus sparked one question after another, and the entire evening passed quickly with the conversation centered around Jesus. As I laid on my bed that night rehearsing what the day had brought I realized I was actually engaged in the assignment Jesus had given me. I was trying to develop a plan to carry out His assignment, while all of the time He was bringing the plan together with normal activities of the day. What a marvellous Person this Jesus was, and how powerful He is to be able to engineer all of the circumstances in others' lives to accomplish His will. I also noted that there were no thoughts of fear during the entire evening, and I reasoned it was because the conversation and my thoughts were focused upon Jesus and not upon myself. As I drifted off to sleep that night a peace came over me that I had not known before. The peace of knowing I had begun my assignment was great.

As I got up from my bed a bitter sweet excitement was in my heart. This was the day I began my new job of outside sales representing the company throughout the region of Decapolis. I was excited with the possibilities that awaited out there, but I was sad with the fact I would be gone from my family for a time. I knew they would be taken care of by friends and neighbors, but I would miss them terribly. As I arrived at the company for last minute instructions the boss unrolled a large map onto the floor. He pointed out the cities he wanted me to visit, and for each city he gave me the name of the person I was to see. Those people were expecting me, and would introduce me to others that were interested in our products. I told him of the offer of lodging at my father-in-law's home, and he was thrilled that it wouldn't cost him for my lodging. As I set out on my journey I was excited to finally be on my way into this new part of my life. However, as I walked out of the city the thoughts began to come to my mind once again of fearful things.

What if the people whom I was to contact had heard about me and my past? What if they didn't want to do business with someone such as me? What if they would not allow me into their businesses or homes for fear that I might harm them? What if I ruined the reputation of my company in that area? What if my boss became the object of ridicule for hiring me in the first place? What if.... What if.... What if...... I tried to think about the job and the purpose of my going, but it seemed to only fuel the negative "what if's."

There was too much at stake to turn back now. Then I began to think about that wonderful day on the shore of the Sea of Galilee at the feet of Jesus and how He simply spoke and the unclean spirit departed from me. He had a look on His face like no other man I had ever seen. I could not describe the difference other than to know it was a look of authority and of peace. He spoke and immediately I felt a peace about me that I had never known before in my entire life, and that peace has lasted until now. So why do I keep thinking negative thoughts? Why is it that whenever something great is happening in my life from God these negative thoughts try to take that peace away from me? I am no longer under the control of the unclean spirit and I have been given an assignment by Jesus to go and tell others what He did for me. To help me accomplish that task, I have been blessed beyond measure. My wife and children have been restored to me in a greater way than ever before. I have new friends that are teaching me about God and this One named Jesus that I personally met. My in-laws have forgiven me and have opened their home to me. I have a better job than I had before which is the method provided for me by God to accomplish my assignment from Jesus.

Then it dawned on me as I walked along the dusty road from Gadara to my in-law's home in Gerasa, that whatever I directed my thoughts towards was what determined the mood I was in. If I allowed all of the negative thoughts of the unclean spirit to take center stage in my mind my mood would become one filled with fear and doubt. If I began to think on all that Jesus had done, and is continuing to do, the peace that I have known returns and I can move forward with each step confident that God will continue to lead me in the way I should go to fulfill my assignment. That means that I am the one who actually controls what I allow to remain in my thoughts, and what I choose to not allow (Philippians 4:8). The answer was there all along but I did not realize it.

The day was cloudy and not so hot so I was covering more miles than I had planned. Thinking on what God had allowed me to see made the time pass quickly, and as daylight began to fade I found myself just outside of the town of Dion. Since it is not safe to travel at night alone on the country roads I decided to spend the night at a friend's home who lived in Dion, and then continue the short journey to Gerasa in the morning. I had not seen my friend in many years, and I hoped he and his family still lived in the same house, and would welcome me for the night. The thought came that he may have heard of what all I had done in my past before I met Jesus and would turn me away; but I dismissed that thought and concentrated on how God had worked everything out to that point and how He would not quit on me now.

I could see light coming through the windows and doorway at my friend's house, and I saw two children playing outside. As I approached the children let out a squeal and ran into the house. Had I scared them? The feeling of fear came again over me, and the thought of turning and going the opposite direction came into my mind. Before I could move I saw a large figure push the curtain aside and stand boldly in the doorway. He asked in an authoritative voice, "Who are you and what do you want"? I called his name and told him who I was. He welcomed me into his home and introduced me to his family. I knew his wife and the oldest of the kids, but the other two children were added since I had last seen them. We shared a delicious meal and joined in as the children played on the floor. When they were all down for the night my friend and I talked for hours. He told me what all had taken place in his life, about the children, his new job, how they were expecting their fourth child in the spring, and some of the challenges that would bring.

Then he asked about me and what all had happened in the years past. I told him about my wife and children, about my job and the promotion I had received as salesman for my company, but I stopped short of telling him the entire story. Once again fear entered into my thoughts. What if I told him and he asked me to leave? What if he feared what I may do to his family? What if...? Then I recalled the conversation I had with myself on the road, and how I can dismiss those negative thoughts with the things of God. After all I did have an assignment from Jesus to tell others what He had done for me, and the compassion He had instead of giving me what I deserved. So, I began from the beginning and told him everything.

Instead of the rejection I feared I found a great interest in what I was telling him. He had never heard of this One called Jesus and was so amazed at what He was able to do. He was fascinated as I told him about the chaos that had developed in my life, and how the words of Jesus brought such a great peace over me. It was as if he couldn't get enough information about Jesus, and he asked me many questions that I could not answer. The next morning as we ate breakfast he shared with his wife what we had discussed, and her interest was very high. Who is this One that can do such things as He did? Who can talk to spirits other than God? As I left, there were hugs all around, and I wanted to stay longer and talk more but I had to go. However, I promised to return since there were people I needed to see in Dion with my job.

It was only a few hours walk from Dion to Gerasa and my in-laws home. The time seemed to be only a matter of a few minutes as I replayed in my head the events of the visit with my friends. Their interest in Jesus was amazing, and I was beginning to get more confidence in my ability to carry out the assignment Jesus had given me to tell others about what He had done. As I arrived at my in-law's home I was greeted with hugs and a meal the likes of which only a mother-in-law can prepare. As we sat and talked my father-in-law told me about the territory I would be dealing with in my job, and how distant some of the cities within the region of Decapolis were. Bethsaida was on the northern shore of the Sea of Galilee, and Raphana was even further north of that in the foothills over forty miles from Gadara. Bethany was forty miles south of Gadara, making the entire area I must cover in my work over eighty miles in length. He suggested using their home as a headquarters when in the southern cities, and going back home to Gadara for the northern cities. I liked the sound of "home." I had only been gone a day and a half, but was missing my family greatly.

I made my first contact that afternoon, and since it was late in the workday I was asked to return the next morning to discuss our products with the owner of a small business who was the contact person my boss had referred. The evening was spent talking about our family and my new job position, but the conversation seemed to always return to Jesus. What little I knew of Him was enough to spark many questions, much more than any of us had answers to.

In the meeting the next morning the owner was excited to be introduced to our new products, and was certain he would be able to incorporate them into his business. After the main sales presentation, and over lunch he asked about my past, where I was from, about my family, and about my relationship with my in-laws who he knew very well and thought of them as fine people. A twinge of nervousness began at the thought of telling him my entire history, but I reminded myself that it was my assignment from Jesus that demanded I tell him everything. As I unfolded the events that led to being under the control of the unclean spirit, the focus shifted from my situation to Jesus. As Jesus became the center of attention the conversation took on new meaning and depth. My client was totally engrossed in this One named Jesus, and had never heard of anyone like Him. He had heard rumors throughout the years that a Messiah was to be born and that He would be from God; but that is all he knew. I listened as he told me things I had never known about Jesus. Were these just rumors or were they really true? The Jews in the synagogue seemed to back up the rumors so there must be some truth to them. I did see Jesus and experienced that miraculous thing of casting out the unclean spirit from me personally. Can anyone do that other than One sent from God Himself? The more we talked the more questions arose. Who is Jesus?

A few days later I found myself in the company of another businessman presenting my products. I was anxious to complete my "sales pitch" and steer the conversation towards Jesus. It seemed as though I now had two main purposes in my job. First was to sell the products our company made, but second was to tell others about Jesus and what He had done for me. When I mentioned the name of Jesus to him I could not believe the reaction it sparked from him. He didn't want to hear any of that "nonsense," and said the things about this man named Jesus were just things the people in the synagogue had started to get people to give more money. He totally dismissed any further conversation about Jesus. I had never had that type of a reaction before and it took me totally by surprise. Who would not want to hear about such a great One as Jesus? After I left and was walking back to my in-law's home I began to consider if the man was right or not. Was Jesus just someone the Jews had invented for their own personal gain? Was I telling others things that were not true? Fear came once again, and I considered the thought of not telling anyone else. If what I was telling others about Jesus was not true I could put my boss and our company in great jeopardy, and we could lose much business. I could be the cause of that, and would most certainly be fired. Should I stop telling others?

Then I began to remember that day on the shore in detail and how Jesus had taken away the thing that was controlling me so completely. It was not a dream or something someone else made up. I had lived it myself and had experienced that deliverance from Jesus personally, and that is something no one can ever take away from me. As I walked and thought the pattern became clear in my mind about what was taking place. I had been given an assignment from Jesus Himself to go home and to my friends, and tell others what Jesus had done for me and how He had compassion towards me instead of judgement. That was the most important thing in my life, and it needs to be that important in the lives of many others.

However, if they never hear how will they know? If they never hear about Jesus they will never have the opportunity to respond to Him (Romans 10:14). It became as clear as the sky above me that it was Satan using the thoughts of the unclean spirit through that man to try to discourage me, and get me to stop telling others about Jesus. Then after my meeting with him I realized that the thoughts of stopping were the work of the unclean spirit of Satan in my own mind seeking that same goal.

The only thing that can really stop me from telling others and carrying out my assignment is me. As the thoughts come into my mind of discouragement and of my own unworthiness I must not allow them to remain. The more I entertain those thoughts the less I am carrying out my assignment, and the more Satan is happy. I have been through so much over the past years, and it all has reinforced in my heart and mind the fact that Satan does not want me telling others about Jesus. I had God's peace return to me as I thought on those things, and did not allow the negative things to remain. There will be difficulties and there will be great opposition from Satan to drag me back to where I was. Even if I never return to the tombs, and if my life with my family and job appear to be well, if I don't tell others about Jesus, Satan will have won the victory in my life.

Every day brought new opportunities not only for sales, but for telling others who had never heard or who had heard strange rumors about Jesus. Most were very eager and thankful to hear, but there were a few who refused to speak about Him. I determined in my heart that was the enemy at work trying to get me to surrender to him, and I would not. The evenings spent in the company of my in-laws were a time of refreshing because they were as interested in Jesus as I was, and maybe even more. Being with those who were as excited about Jesus as I was became a source of encouragement for me for the next day. Throughout my stay in that region I made many contacts for sales, and I followed up on many new referrals that seemed to come from some unseen sources. The conversation about Jesus became more detailed as I learned things others had heard about Him, and could pass that information along. Sales were good and orders were being placed, which meant my presence in that area was very profitable for my company. I knew my boss would be thrilled with the results, and that would insure my presence in that area for a long time to come. From my perspective the opportunities to continue to share what Jesus did for me would continue and even expand. I could see God working in my life to keep me in contact with new people, as well as encourage those who had heard.

Many months passed and many people had heard about Jesus from me. Those who heard told others, and the name of Jesus was becoming known everywhere I went. From Raphana in the north to Bethany in the south the name of Jesus was known. There were still those who did not want to hear, but they were becoming fewer and fewer as the name of Jesus became more well known. What a joy it was for me to realize I had been faithful to my assignment, and God had blessed. Had I listened to the unclean spirit which brought fear and confusion it never would have happened, and the name of Jesus would have been unknown. The unclean spirit never stops its attack on me, but I have learned what to do when it comes. It increases in intensity, and is harder to resist; but as I recognize what is going on I can counter it with thoughts of Jesus.

One day I was in Bethsaida going about my work when I noticed a commotion over by the seashore. Crowds of people were rushing down the hill to see something, but I could not see what. As I made my way to the shore I saw in the distance the One I thought I would never see again. It was Jesus standing in the middle of a great crowd. They had brought one that was deaf (Mark 7:31-37) to Him to be healed, and He did. Just as Jesus had removed the unclean spirit from me, He healed the deaf man who could now hear the wonderful words of Jesus. That triggered a massive amount of people rushing towards Him with those who were sick, or had some physical ailment to be healed.

How did all of these people know who Jesus was? He had never visited this area before and there was nothing said about His coming. Could it be that as I told people about what Jesus had done for me that they remembered? My heart was thrilled with the thought that I may have had something to do with the deaf man being healed. In a very small way, yet a very necessary way, the assignment Jesus had given me had a purpose. Others needed to hear of the loving compassion He had on me so they could also seek Him, and find the same peace that was given to me.

It became very clear that the only thing that could show others the love God has for them is me telling them what He did for me. The only thing that can stop others from hearing is me listening to the unclean spirit trying to stop me by discouraging me with lies. Seeing the crowds of people around Jesus that day gave me a sense of wanting to know more about Him, so I could tell even more people of His love for them. As I thought about these things I had an overwhelming sense of unworthiness, and the thought that I am not good enough to be telling others about Jesus flooded over me. I don't know enough to be telling anyone anything so important as the things of God. Why do I think anyone would listen to me, the one who was so very much out of control? What if I give wrong information to the people I talk to, and they go a wrong way because of me? This time however, I stopped the thoughts and realized that Satan never stops trying to get me to give up on my assignment. The unclean spirit is placing lies and negative, confusing thoughts into my mind at such a rapid rate I can hardly recognize one thought from the other.

The thoughts of stopping only increased my determination to gain more knowledge of Jesus so I could tell more people. I have learned that I can control what I allow to remain in my thoughts, and what I eliminate out of my mind (Philippians 4:8-9). I now know that entertaining the thoughts from the unclean spirit will eventually lead me back to the tombs, and back to my former lifestyle of addiction. If for no other reason than my sweet family I must not allow those thoughts to remain for even the smallest amount of time (Ephesians 4:27).

I wanted to see Jesus and let Him know that I had been faithful to His assignment; so, I began to make my way down the hill towards Him. The crowds of people were difficult to move through, and there was much pushing and shoving to get closer to Him, but I managed to get within a small distance from Him. Then I was pushed from behind, and I lost my footing on the grass and fell to my knees. I struggled to stand up, and when I did I saw Jesus standing in the middle of a crowd but He was looking directly at me. I could not get any closer to Him, so I called out His name. Immediately a smile came to His face and the slightest nod of His head told me that He recognized me, and that He was well pleased with my faithfulness in following His leading to help me continue with my assignment.

With that smile of approval, I suddenly realized it was Jesus who had opened the way for me to be reunited with my family by working in my wife and children's hearts. It was Jesus who had given my in-laws the spirit of forgiveness I so desperately needed. It was Jesus who allowed the company I worked for to grow, and have need of a salesman in the area where Jesus wanted me to tell others. It was Jesus who placed the desire to hire me back into the heart and mind of my boss. It was Jesus who opened the hearts of those I spoke to about Him, and gave them a desire to know more. It was Jesus who did all things for me to allow me to carry out His assignment of going and telling others about Him.

With the smile of Jesus, I also realized that there is an enemy who is just as determined to stop me. Through the voice of the unclean spirit in my mind, Satan places confusing images in the right place at the right time for me to consider. The attacks from Satan through the unclean spirit will be with me the rest of my life, but I do not need to heed them. I need to measure them by the unchanging standard of God's Word, and not the unstableness of my own feelings (1 John 4:1 *Beloved, believe not every spirit, but try the spirits whether they are of God: because many false prophets are gone out into the world.*).

One other thing I realized was that I am not alone in the battle with the unclean spirit. Every human being on the face of the earth is influenced by the unclean spirit doing its best to keep them from learning the truth of God through Jesus Christ. While Satan's power is greater than anything I can ever control on my own, the power of Jesus living in and through me is greater than anything the unclean spirit can try to tempt me with (1 John 4:4 Ye *are of God, little children, and have overcome them: because greater is he that is in you, than he that is in the world.*). The more knowledge I have of Jesus the more I will know truth which will help me identify the untruth; the lies that the unclean spirit is trying to get me to believe.

I finished my trip and returned home to hugs and kisses, and some much-needed down time with my family. While I was gone my wife had met some people who gathered together once a week to discuss Jesus and the things of God. That is exactly what I was looking for, someone who could teach me more about Jesus, and how I can live for Him better.

The next day we went to the meeting place and found several people I knew, including one of the men I worked with at our company and his family. I was very surprised at his being there since he was one of the men that talked me into the beginning of my troubles. When I expressed my surprise, he asked me to step outside so he could explain without interrupting the rest of the group. He apologized in no uncertain terms for his actions in influencing me to do wrong. While I was working with the guys as a part of my training I would often speak of my experience, and how Jesus is the only One who could set me free. He was listening, and God was working on his heart during that time. When I left to begin my new sales job, he prayed and placed his trust in Jesus as his Saviour. He also began telling his wife and children about what he had done and how Jesus was the One who made the change in his life also. As we spoke he told me that it was because of me simply doing the assignment Jesus had given me to tell others that he learned how to change the direction his life was going.

As we stood there, a sense of accomplishment came over me that felt very good. Many times, I had told others about Jesus when the opportunity was there, but this one time I was able to see the results of obeying. We went back inside and the discussion was sweet. There were several men with their wives, and several ladies whose husbands were not interested. As we ended our time we prayed for them to realize the forgiveness available in Jesus alone. As my family and I walked back to our house I had a renewed enthusiasm to tell others about Jesus, and I was very anxious to learn more. God has been so very good to me by guiding my life through all of the problems, and yet still loving me and blessing me and my family. It is such a wonderful thing to serve Jesus Christ.

Chapter 11 A Final Word

If I could sum up all that I learned throughout my journey in life and tell it to you, what would I say? There is so much more I could have written, but the main things I wanted you to realize have been covered. The most important thing would be to let you know that Jesus loves you with a love you cannot even imagine, regardless of what you have done in your past.

The things that you allowed into your life were all things God used to get you to a place in your life where you would be willing to listen to Him, and begin to take Him seriously. God does not want you to be involved in evil, sinful things; but when you do He will use the consequences of those things to show you His love if you will allow Him to. Like with me, sometimes the consequences of your actions may be severe such as illness or even incarceration. When you don't respond to God's direction in your life these things are the only way for Him to get your attention. It is like a child who does wrong, and the parents who are willing to go to great lengths to show him the right way.

Genesis 50:20 *But as for you, ye thought evil against me; but God meant it unto good...*

The starting place for true and lasting deliverance from the unclean things that control you is to humble yourself before Him, just as I did when I ran to Jesus and knelt at His feet. In my heart I was letting go of every attempt to control my sin, and let Jesus take it and forgive me of it. I cannot do anything on my own to pay the price that must be paid to God for the sin I have committed. Only Jesus Christ can make that payment, and He did. All that is required from you is to place your trust in what Jesus has already done for you, and then allow Him to lead in your life. Without His forgiveness you will remain in your sin, and you will be accountable for it to God both in this life, and throughout all eternity.

Romans 10:9 *That if thou shalt confess with thy mouth the Lord Jesus, and shalt believe in thine heart that God hath raised him from the dead, thou shalt be saved.*

The second thing I wish to show you is that Satan, the enemy of God, will try to get you to doubt God's leadership and direction in your life and he never quits as long as you are alive. Placing your trust in Jesus Christ to save you makes you a child of God. In Jesus you are greatly loved by God even more than a parent loves their child. Satan cannot hurt God so he goes after the object of God's love, His child.

The attack of Satan is nothing new and nothing unique to you. It all began back in the garden of Eden when Satan got Eve to doubt what God had commanded.

God told Adam, (Genesis 2:17) *But of the tree of the knowledge of good and evil, thou shalt not eat of it: for in the day that thou eatest thereof thou shalt surely die.*

Satan told Eve, (Genesis 3:4) *And the serpent said unto the woman, Ye shall not surely die:*

Satan's lies have never stopped since that day, and they never will stop coming to you as long as you are alive. You don't hear an audible voice telling you these things, but rather Satan puts thoughts into your mind for you to consider. Satan and his demons communicate with you through the unclean spirit. Jesus identified it in me when He first saw me.

Mark 5:2 *And when he [Jesus] was come out of the ship, immediately there met him out of the tombs a man with an unclean spirit...*

The unclean spirit placed evil, selfish, sinful thoughts into my mind and I allowed them to remain by considering them. At first, I knew they were wrong and yet I questioned in my heart if they might be true. When I did that I opened the door for the unclean spirit to control my life, and it did (Mark 5:1-20). Jesus cast out the unclean spirit, but it wasn't long before it was back trying to get me confused and quit serving God. When I listened to what was being suggested to me in my thoughts I was discouraged, confused, depressed, and seriously considered going back to my old ways. However, when I realized what the unclean spirit was trying to do, control my life once again, I would replace those thoughts with God's truth (Philippians 4:8-9), and be back on track.

The way to know when the unclean spirit is trying to gain entrance into your life is to know the Word of God, the Bible. If you know truth you will know when something is wrong.

John 8:32 *And ye shall know the truth, and the truth shall make you free.*

The third and last thing I want you to know is that you cannot win the battle on your own. God never intended you to fight the battles against the unclean spirit by yourself. God gave me the support I needed to stay on the right track, and not look back from my family as well as from the group of people who met together to talk about Jesus and learn more of God's ways. Today this is called the church, and it is the support group God has given you to help and encourage you to succeed in your battle. When God created the first man, Adam, He made the statement that it was not good for man to be alone (Genesis 2:18).

If I were to go to battle with an enemy all by myself I would soon be defeated. However, if I took with me a powerful army of others who are battling the same battle as I am, victory would be much more assured. God has placed many Bible teaching churches in your area, and has one that is where He wants you to learn and serve. Just as a loving parent provides all of the "tools" and encouragement for their child to mature and be successful, so does God our heavenly Father. He provides His written Word the Bible, a way to communicate with Him in prayer; and the encouragement and teaching we need in the church to grow our faith and be victorious in our daily battle with the unclean spirit.

It does take more than just "praying to God you never come back to this place." It takes work and dedication on your part to follow Jesus regardless of the cost. Simply follow Jesus!

Your fellow soldier in Christ,
James

Introduction

The term "recidivism" refers to the cycle of arrest, release, and re-arrest. However, the term can be applied to returning to any former behavior. The Merriam-Webster dictionary defines recidivism as, "*a tendency to relapse into a previous condition or mode of behavior; especially relapse into criminal behavior.*" Not only could it apply to a return to criminal behavior and incarceration, but also applies to the return to an addiction.

An addiction is anything that controls you physically, mentally, or spiritually.

As was stated in section 1, not all addictions are bad.

1 Corinthians 16:15 ... *ye know the house of Stephanas, that it is the firstfruits of Achaia, and that they have **addicted** themselves to the ministry of the saints* (Emphasis mine.)

Paul is describing the actions and attitude of the household of Stephanas as being "*addicted... to the ministry of the saints.*" In other words, what was controlling their thoughts, actions, attitudes, and their entire purpose, was the ministry of believers in Jesus Christ. This included personal devotion to Christ through prayer, Bible study, and church participation, as well as seeing to the needs of individual believers both physically, emotionally, and spiritually. God's Word claims they were "addicts," but in a very good sense.

Today, when we think of the word "addict" or "addiction" we think first of substance abuse, such as alcohol or illegal drug use. However, an addiction is not limited to these things. An addiction can be an uncontrolled temper or anger, the pursuit of pleasure, an obsession with sports, an unbalanced work ethic, eating disorders, tobacco usage, pornography, as well as drugs and alcohol. While treatment programs abound, especially in the United States, most do not identify the root of an addiction and stop it. Treatment programs can furnish a great number of suggested life-style changes to help a person once they are free from their addiction, but unless the very root of the addiction is address, it will be returned to. This can be termed as "recidivism."

What is the root of all addictions? God's Word is very clear as to the source of things that control us, other than the Spirit of God.

Mark 5:1-2 *And they came over unto the other side of the sea, into the country of the Gadarenes. (2) And when he [Jesus] was come out of the ship, immediately there met him out of the tombs a man with **an unclean spirit**,* (emphasis mine)

An "unclean spirit" is how Satan and his demons communicate with you and me, through our thoughts. The man who is the object of Jesus' compassion in Mark 5:1-20, commonly known as the "demoniac of Gadara," is seen to have every characteristic of an addict; one who is being controlled physically, mentally, or spiritually, or as with this man, controlled in all those areas. When Jesus approached him, He did not proclaim that he was a man who was sick with an illness, or that he was a man who inherited his father's family traits. Jesus stated firmly, and without any hesitation or analysis, that he was a "man with an unclean spirit."

As you read the passages in Mark 5:1-20 you will notice that many other people had tried to bind him with chains and fetters (leg restraints), and could not. He would break them apart and walk away. The chains and fetters were put on him in an attempt to restrain him and alter his behavior. However, unless the root of the behavior is addressed and changed, it is similar to placing a bandage on a broken arm and waiting for it to heal. The source of his problem was the fact that he was listening to, and heeding the unclean spirit; the voice of Satan and his demons as they placed thoughts into his mind. Man cannot control or order Satan and his demons into doing anything, since they are much more powerful than humans. But Jesus Christ, the Son of God and God the Son can, and does.

Jesus not only identified the source of this man's torment immediately; but when the man humbled himself before Jesus, He ordered the demons from him and his torment and anguish ceased immediately. Jesus didn't tell him to enter into a lengthy program, or "pray through," or do anything at all that he had not already done. He admitted his problem and humble himself before Jesus. The unclean spirit was removed immediately; and a great peace and longing to be with Jesus filled him. Jesus gave him an assignment as seen in Mark 5:19.

Mark 5:19 *Howbeit Jesus suffered him not, but saith unto him, Go home to thy friends, and tell them how great things the Lord hath done for thee, and hath had compassion on thee.*

He was to return to his family and friends and let them know what Jesus had done for him. In Mark 5:20, we see that he faithfully carried out that assignment.

Mark 5:20 *And he departed, and began to publish in Decapolis how great things Jesus had done for him: and all men did marvel.*

This is all that is recorded in God's Word about this man whom Jesus had compassion on by delivering him from the control of the unclean spirit. In section 2 you were introduced to this man, and what *could have* happened to him on his journey to complete the assignment given to him by Jesus. As his story unfolds, one thing is very clear. While the unclean spirit does not *possess* a person who has placed their trust in Jesus Christ as their Saviour, it does constantly try to *control* that person's thoughts and actions, and sidetrack him from Jesus' love and purpose for them. The story of how he may have carried out his assignment from Jesus is based upon biblical principles that apply to each one of us, and how we can avoid being swayed away from our God-given purpose.

Recidivism is the return to any former behavior, and that is what this book considers through the life of the former "demoniac of Gadara," now known simply as James. The lessons to be learned are very hard lessons for the one who returns to his or her "old ways," and it is the aim of this book to reveal and demonstrate how the unclean spirit constantly and subtly attacks the mind with thoughts that are self-centered and totally opposite to Christ.

Proverbs 8:10 *Receive my instruction, and not silver; and knowledge rather than choice gold.*

Chaplain Tim Klink

Chapter 12   Freedom

In section 2, I introduced myself, but please, allow me to do it again and bring you up to date on my life. Even though my name is not recorded in the Bible, I do have a name. It is a name most people in your part of the world cannot pronounce or even spell, so you can just call me James. Even though there are many different people named James recorded in the Bible, I am not one of them. I am now forty years old, and have lived in the vicinity of Gadara all of my life. I have family and relatives living throughout the region of Decapolis, and I know the country very well. I was employed at a trade which I enjoyed very much, and I don't mind telling you, was very good at.

My lovely wife has given me four amazing children whom I love with all of my heart and are growing up too quickly. The littlest one could write a book on all of the ways a child can get into trouble, but always in a creative way. He is never mean, just cute. One day he will grow up to be a natural leader of men. His love and compassion to the other children continues to grow and develop, and I can see the possibilities in his life beginning to take shape. The other three are maturing, and it is a joyous time to watch how they are growing physically, as well as emotionally and spiritually.

My beautiful wife is still the love of my life. Even though we met and married when we were very young, she is still my trusted best friend, and companion for life. The love we have for each other grows and deepens as the years pass. Besides that, she is still the greatest cook one could ever know. One might look at my life and be very jealous with all of the blessings I have been given.

I worked with a group of guys that were a little "rough around the edges," to say the least. I began to listen to them, and the thought became more prominent in my mind that I needed more "me" time. While I enjoyed my family greatly, I just knew there was something missing in my life, so I made one of the stupidest decisions ever in my life. I decided to start hanging out with them after work and on weekends, which was over the objections of my wife and kids.

Things progressed quickly with these guys, and it wasn't long before I was participating in activities, and going places that I would have never imagined. It was not long before my wife gave me the ultimatum to either stop my actions, or move out of the house for the sake of the kids.

I went from one "friends" house to another, but soon wore out my welcome everywhere. I had reached the bottom of my life when I moved into the tombs that are in the hills outside of Gadara. That was a wicked place, where there was no law. Not only were the tombs places where dead people are buried, they are also places where a person can lose their life for something as simple as a coat. It was a terrifying place, and only the strongest survived.

As I sank deeper into the things that were controlling me, I became one of the strongest men there. Others feared me, so I was left somewhat alone. This thing that I started out considering in my life, what I thought was a new "freedom," was now controlling me. I loved it while at the same time I hated it greatly.

As time progressed, it became apparent that I had no control over my thoughts and actions, and was totally controlled by something I feared greatly. I would look at myself in a morning and find that I was covered in blood. It was my blood from all of the cutting this thing inside me had led me to do. There were times when men would come and try to put chains on me to tame my actions, but my strength was now so great that I snapped the iron chains like paper. During rare moments of being able to think somewhat clearly, I would cry for deliverance from this thing inside of me, this monster I had allowed to take over my life. But things only got worse and I knew that the only relief I would ever find would be in death.

I sat on the hillside outside of the tombs one sunny morning, overlooking the Sea of Galilee. The sky was a beautiful blue and the air smelled cleaner than I remembered. The night before, a terrible storm passed through, but it seemed to have cleaned things up, and I was enjoying a very peaceful moment. There were fishing boats on the water as there were most days. As I watched, one of the larger fishing ships was headed straight for the shore and landed. That was a dangerous thing, since no one ever landed on this stretch of beach, fearing us who lived in the tombs.

A man got out and stood there looking straight at me. It was as if He was not just looking at me, but was looking into me. His gaze drew me to Him, and I began to run to Him with a longing for deliverance inside of me that I had never felt before. As I knelt before Him and sobbed, He began to speak to the thing that was inside of me, commanding it to depart out of me. All of a sudden, the pigs on the other hillside began to squeal loudly, and they all ran over a cliff and drowned in the sea. Immediately, I felt a peace I had not known in many years come over me. Whoever this man was, He had accomplished what I desired more than life itself- inner peace. I was free at last from the monster that controlled me!

My desire was to be with Him and to go with Him when He got back into the ship. But He told me to go back home and tell my friends what He had done for me and what great compassion God had shown to me. As He and the others with Him sailed away I just sat on the shore watching until they were out of sight. Going home didn't seem to be an option, but going back to the tombs was definitely not something I desired to do.

As I walked towards home, thoughts poured into my mind about what might await me. The thoughts of my family, and especially by dear wife, were overwhelming; but the thoughts of rejection and hurt that may be waiting for me were just as demanding. I kept walking as I weighed what the right thing was to do, and soon I was at the doorway of my house. To my pleasant surprise, my family welcomed me, having noticed the change in me.

The things I experienced in my mind as I determined to follow the assignment given to me by Jesus to go home and tell others, is without a doubt the same things you are going through in your life. I don't wish to repeat what is in section 2, but rather, take you beyond where that section ends.

I was promoted to outside sales at the company, and soon I had travelled the entire region of Decapolis with the mission of telling as many people as I could what all Jesus had done for me, in addition to selling our products. My family was involved in a gathering of other believers in Jesus, and we were all growing in our knowledge of God as a family. Sales were skyrocketing, which meant my income was very good. My life was better than I ever remembered it to be.

I have to deal with the unclean spirit on a moment by moment basis as it tries to get me to become side-tracked from the things of God. One of the greatest, and most successful deceptions Satan uses is to get you to believe he is not there. He speaks to your thoughts through the unclean spirit, and tries to get you to believe it is your thoughts, not his. And he never gives up...*ever*!

Chapter 13   Success

During the next few months, the demand for our products in the region of Decapolis grew at a tremendous pace. More outside sales people were added to the company to keep up with demand, and I was promoted to sales manager. I often think back to where I had been, living in the tombs, separated from family and friends, and being controlled by Satan's demons through the unclean spirit. I pray to God I never go back to that place again!

With my new responsibilities comes more work, and just like you, there are never enough hours in a day to keep ahead. I know that my time with my family is very precious, and I guard it the best that I can. The kids are getting involved with social things now and they are facing issues that need my advice and direction as their Dad. As these issues develop in their lives, it places added stress on my wife who must deal with them when I am gone. It seems like I am gone more than I am home with the new position.

I have tried to think of how I could get more accomplished in my day, and have arrived at the conclusion that I cannot do it all. Something is going to have to go. My job is so very important because it is supplying us with the funds to buy the things we have always desired. And now with the kids growing older, they need more space. We have been considering purchasing a larger house, but that will take considerably more than I am currently making.

The opportunity is there for higher wages, but it requires putting in even more time to my job. The problem is that I am already stretched to the limit. I work six days a week. Two evenings per week we meet with our Christian group to study God's Word. My wife and I have reserved one night per week as a "date night," and we spend the remaining nights with the kids. I get up early in the morning and I think about God's Word and pray, and before I go to bed I meditate on what I have heard in our gathering of believers and pray for my family.

As I thought on the situation, I began to consider taking just one early morning, and instead of having my quiet time with God, get a head start on the day's work. After all, what would one day a week hurt? I am meeting with God the other six days. So that's what I did. I took one morning each week and jumped right into my work. I did say a quick prayer, but it was simply to satisfy my conscience, and meant very little. While I did get much work done that day, the next day produced even more work that buried me.

Before long, I was working three mornings, and having a very limited quiet time with God, which didn't really mean much. I kept justifying myself with the thought that "God gave me the work; therefore, I need to give it all I can to be a 'good steward' for God." Deep inside me, I knew I was only fooling myself, and that God didn't want me working instead of spending time with Him. But I allowed my thoughts to overrule what I knew to be right.

The next week I had the largest increase in sales volume I ever had. My early mornings of work were great for getting all of the extra paperwork finished. God was truly blessing my life with the extra income, as well as the popularity I now had with the boss. Also, the guys in the shop welcomed all of the overtime they were asked to do to keep up with the demand. They still had their time of "fun" when they were not working, and there was always a standing invitation to join them.

As the months passed, I found myself working more and more hours, and spending less time with my family and my Bible study group. I kept justifying it by telling myself this was what God had given me to do, and I must take care of it. I could not understand why my wife and kids could not see how hard I was working for their future. I knew I was a good husband and Dad, but they kept nagging me about the time I spent away from them.

The one man at work that is a part of our Bible study group kept bugging me to get back into the group. He should have known, of all people, how demanding my job had become. After all, it was my sales efforts that provided him with a great income. Why didn't he see that? I was sacrificing my family time so he could have it comfortable. Every time I saw him coming up to me, I would find somewhere else to be so I wouldn't have to listen to him. After all, I'm okay in my relationship with Jesus and God. I really don't need to be in the

Bible study every time they meet. I know enough of God's Word that I don't need to read it every day. I'm okay!

There was a part of me that was continually "high" on the fast pace of the work, and another part of me that was absolutely exhausted from it. But the voice inside my head kept driving me on, and encouraging me to take on more and more projects. At that point I wasn't certain what I wanted, but one thing I knew was that I needed to find more time to fit in all of the work I was committed to.

And then the day came that my wife informed me that we were expecting another baby. You talk about mixed emotions! Having another little one running around the house would be such a joy, especially since the other kids are getting older. The fun we used to have in the evenings together playing, or just hanging out together in the yard watching the stars would be nice to have again. But reality quickly set in, knowing I didn't have time for another child. I hardly had enough time to see the kids I have now. The demands of a baby are great, and I just don't think I can handle it right now. But she is pregnant, and like it or not, the baby is on its way.

I began to think about the size of our house, and how it barely holds all of us now that the kids are older. We will need a bigger house, or at the very least, add on to the one we have. That all costs money that we don't have. I will need to take on more work to be able to provide what my growing family will need. How am I ever going to do that? I am almost to the breaking point now.

I was in my office at the company working late on a Friday night, when several of the men from the factory came in and invited me to go get something to eat with them. I didn't need to stay long, and I did need to eat something since I had worked right through lunch. I remembered the times I had spent with them that started all of my problems, but I reasoned within myself that I was stronger now. After all, I am a Christian and I can handle any temptation that may present itself. I was very hungry, so I agreed to go with them, but only for a very short time. I still had several hours of work yet that night.

They went to one of the old places they had taken me before. The place brought back memories that I really wanted to forget, but I remembered that the food was great, and I was starved. As we sat and talked, the smell of the food cooking mixed with other smells began to bring a degree of comfort to me. It was like visiting an old friend, but I knew in my heart that I should not have been there. After several hours had passed I excused myself and told the men I needed to get back to the office. As I walked out, I prided myself on the fact that all I did was eat my food, and didn't partake of anything that was wrong. I knew I was a strong enough follower of Jesus to overcome any temptation that was there.

My supper break caused me to come home very late, and needless to say, my wife was not happy. The kids were all in bed and she just looked at me. The cat even avoided me that evening. I could see the concern in her eyes that I had seen before when I got into all of the trouble with those same guys. It seemed as if she wanted to hit me, hug me, or just stand there and cry. I wasn't sure how to read her. I hadn't done anything wrong, so I just blamed her emotions on the fact that she was a pregnant lady.

Over the course of the next few weeks, it became a habit of spending evenings with the guys for a supper break. My wife went from being concerned to being angry, and then to the silent treatment. Down inside of her heart, she was scared that I was slipping back to where I had come from. I tried to assure her it was just supper and nothing more, but she had a very difficult time believing me.

As I sat with the guys one very hot evening, they offered me a drink that they said would cool me down and go good with the supper. I hesitated, but then I reasoned within myself that I was strong enough to handle one drink. It would really taste good on such a hot night, so I agreed. After the meal, and finishing late at the office I went home. What I didn't realize was that the smell of that drink went right along with me, and my wife noticed it the moment I walked in the room. She was furious!

I didn't need her telling me what I could and couldn't do. I am the head of the house, and the decisions I make should be accepted without question. I work long, hard hours at my job, and a little "me time" is what helps me get things done. If one little drink helps with that, who is she to complain? That evening was difficult to say the least. We both went to bed silently. The next morning was just a continuation of the night before- silence.

The times spent over the supper breaks with the guys became longer and longer, to the point that I didn't go back to the office to finish what I was working on. Of course, I told my wife that I did. Without realizing it, I was headed back to the old ways once again.

Chapter 14 Failure

Success can be a wonderful thing, or it can tear your life apart. It wasn't long before the relationship with my wife was back to where it had been. My kids were upset with me for not treating their Mom kindly like I used to do, as well as never being home much anymore. I reasoned within myself that it was much better to just stay away, than to face the constant nagging from my wife.

I thought about how this same scenario developed several years ago, which ended up with me living in the tombs. The thing that made the difference in my life then was Jesus, and that wonderful day I met Him on the shore. I know the answer is to return to Him in my heart and life, but how can He ever forgive me? He took the unclean spirit out of me once, and now I am treating that as if it were not important in my life. I have done too much bad stuff for Him to ever love me again like He did.

Since that was my attitude, things only got worse. My work didn't seem to have a purpose anymore, and I got farther and farther behind. I would get subtle looks from the boss every time I was around the office, so I tried to avoid being there, which only made matters worse. I spent as much time as I could in the evenings and on weekends with the guys, and after a while it didn't seem to matter if I went home or not. My life was headed down faster than a speeding camel on a sand dune.

Things became unbearable at home, so most nights, I didn't even bother to go there. I knew my wife needed me there, especially since she was pregnant, but I just couldn't take her attitude towards me. She just didn't understand my need for "me time." She thinks everything should revolve around her and the new baby, but that just isn't fair to me. I love her very much, but I can't handle being around her when she has that type of an attitude. So, I avoid her most of the time.

I don't understand why I am going down this same path as before. I am a Christian and I considered myself as a strong Christian. If Jesus loved me so much, as I thought He did, why is He bringing all of this bad stuff back into my life? Why doesn't He stop it? Doesn't He know it is all wrong? He simply doesn't care anymore because I have gone too far this time. I have crossed some "line" that must never be crossed to stay in Jesus' good graces. I want to get back to Him, but I don't think He wants me back.

One day while I was working in the office, the boss came in, shut the door, and sat down across from me. I could tell by the look on his face that this was not a social visit. Over the next hour we had a "heart to heart" talk, which resulted in a very kind, but firm, ultimatum. Either straighten up and focus, or step down. I had sensed that was coming, but when it actually arrived, I was at a loss for words. Just the thought of losing my job at this point in my life was a devastating thought. The kids were growing older and needed things, my wife was pregnant with our fifth child, we needed a larger house for all to fit, and I was having a terrible time focusing on my work.

The voice inside of me was encouraging me to not make such a big deal out of it. After all, I was very talented in what I do, and I should have no trouble getting another job. If losing my job is how God cares about me, then I can live without Him. I hated that attitude, and I knew it wasn't right; but I was so angry with everything, that was all I could think about.

Not going home most nights developed into not going home at all. I was never asked outright to move out, it just seemed to be the easiest thing to do. The guys allowed me once again to crash at their places until I wore out my welcome with them. Since I was still working, I found a small place of my own and rented it. With keeping the bills paid at home, plus the added expense of a place of my own, it was tight to say the least. My wife was not able to earn any money since she was pregnant, so the entire expense was upon me.

With a place of my own, I could bring work home with me and begin to get caught up with the projects I had been assigned. Going out with the guys in the evenings became more difficult to afford so that slowed down greatly. It seemed like I was headed in a right direction, if I could just stay focused on what was the most important thing, my work.

A week or so later I decided I needed to visit with all of our outside salesmen throughout Decapolis that worked under me. That would give me a time away from everything that was happening in my life, and allow me to focus entirely on my work. As I packed for the trip, excitement began to grow within me of what all could be accomplished with these visits. I had not been to many of the regions since I took over as general sales manager. A change of scenery would be good.

I headed south of Gadara to my friend's home in Dion, where I had spent a night with him and his family on my first sales trip. As I approached his house, I saw him sitting under a tree reading something on a small scroll. When I called his name he looked up, and before I knew it he had placed a big hug on me right there in the front yard. It was so good to see him again, and to have a friendly face to look at.

After the evening meal we went outside into the cool evening air and sat for what seemed like hours. I unloaded upon him all that had been going on in my life since I last saw him. The look of concern on his face was very genuine as I told him of my problems at home, as well as at work. When I had finished laying everything out for him, he then told me what was happening in his life and with his family.

We spoke briefly about his job and how his family had grown, but then he told me about the impact my first visit had upon their lives as I shared Jesus with them. After I left on that first visit, they told several of their friends and relatives about what I said concerning Jesus, and they began meeting regularly to search the scriptures to see if what was said was really true about Him. He told me that the more they searched and spoke to others who heard things about Him, the more they were convinced that Jesus truly was the Messiah they had been waiting for. They each placed their trust in Jesus to save them through His death of the cross, and His resurrection from the dead. The more they searched the scriptures, the more they discovered that was all foretold about Him.

My friend then asked me what was probably the most embarrassing question I had ever been asked. He asked how the group I was meeting with was doing. At that moment all I felt like doing was getting up and running. How could I tell him that I had not met with them for many months, and that I had returned to my old ways? How could I tell him that I had not read the scriptures in almost that same length of time? How could I tell him that I was angry with God for causing all of the problems in my life?

Then I did something I had not done in a very long time; I began to cry. Tears welled up in my eyes and I felt as if my chest would explode with emotion. I was so ashamed at what I had allowed to come into my life. I finally realized that the root of all of the problems that had occurred in my life was of my own making. The same unclean spirit that had me living in those awful tombs, among those violent people, was the same unclean spirit that I had allowed back into my life. I remembered listening to it as it told me that I needed a break from my work, and that going out with the guys again would be the relaxation I needed. It all made sense!

Chapter 15   Restoration

How could I ever go back to God after I turned my back on Him? If I were God, I would not have anything to do with me. As I tried to explain my feelings to my friend, he picked up the small scroll he was reading when I first arrived, and turned to a portion that he read to me.

Jeremiah 3:22 *Return, ye backsliding children, and I will heal your backslidings. Behold, we come unto thee; for thou art the LORD our God.*

How could Jesus love me and want me back after all I have done? This scripture must be speaking about someone else; surely it cannot apply to me. My friend told me that I had not lost my salvation because I had never done anything to earn it in the first place. Jesus had done everything needed by paying for all of my sin with His sinless blood on the cross. When He came out of the grave alive, it was proof that God the Father had accepted Jesus' sacrifice as payment for my sin.

My friend then asked me what I do when one of my children does something wrong. I told him that I correct them. He answered with the question, "What do you do if they don't obey your correction? Do you kick them out of the family and disown them?" Of course, I wouldn't; they are my kids. He explained that is exactly our relationship with God because of what Jesus had done for us. God doesn't kick us out of His family, but He does correct us. I thought back on how many times I had to allow my oldest son to realize for himself that what he was doing was wrong, and yet I still loved him regardless of what the issue was.

It all seemed so wonderful that Jesus could forgive me, because He never stopped loving me. I realized that my relationship with Him was strained, just as it was when my son was disobeying my guidance, and that it may be able to be restored. But how is that possible? What do I have to do? My friend then rolled his way down through the scroll to another passage and read it to me.

Jeremiah 4:1 *If thou wilt return, O Israel, saith the LORD, return unto me: and if thou wilt put away thine abominations out of my sight, then shalt thou not remove.*

He explained to me that this was written by the prophet Jeremiah to the nation of Israel who had turned away from worshipping God, and began to worship idols. Just as the nation of Israel had listened to the unclean spirit in their lives, and had obeyed the lies that Satan and his demons were telling them to keep them from God's love and blessings, so it was with me. The things that are written in the scriptures are a document of how God deals with all of mankind. Since these things are about God, they never change, because God never changes (Malachi 3:6).

My friend went on to point out to me that God began in Jeremiah 4:1 with the word "if." That is a word that requires something from me to be able to receive what God has promised. I must return to the Lord to be able to receive His blessing of forgiveness. I thought of how long I had stayed away from Him after He had done so very much for me. Jesus had delivered me from the control of the unclean spirit that beautiful day on the shore of the Sea of Galilee. Jesus had allowed me to identify the attempts of the unclean spirit to bring me back into its lies, and gave me victory over it. Jesus had restored my family to me, and had shown me others that believed just as I did. Jesus allowed me to have the job as outside sales so I could tell others what He had done for me. It was all Jesus, and it was all good blessings.

It became very clear to me that I had, once again, fallen into the trap of the unclean spirit, and had listened to his lies. The unclean spirit was telling me that I needed to find pleasure and comfort in my life when I had it all the time through Jesus and His blessings. How stupid was that? I had proven once again in my life that Satan is very subtle, and if I am not watching every moment of the day, the lies of the unclean spirit will deceive me.

But now that I have messed up everything with my family and with my job once again, how can it ever be made right? What do I need to do to get back to where I was with Jesus? My friend once again pointed out to me the next "if" in Jeremiah 4:1.

Jeremiah 4:1 *If thou wilt return, O Israel, saith the LORD, return unto me: and if thou wilt put away thine abominations out of my sight, then shalt thou not remove.*

I must put away the things that have drawn me away from God. The time spent with the guys was an attempt to find some pleasure and fun in my life that cost me almost everything again, and I need to stop. The obsession with my work needed to stop also. I have to work to be able to pay the bills, but work cannot be the driving force in my life. It must have its place in perspective to God and my family. These are the things that are the "abominations" in my life that have come between me and God.

I told my friend that I didn't understand why God didn't answer my prayers anymore. I had prayed to God that He would get me back with my family and get my wife to understand me better. I had prayed that my work would be successful like it was before, but things only got worse. Why didn't God answer my prayer? Since God didn't hear me and answer me, I knew that He didn't care for me and had written me off.

As I began to pour this all out to my friend, he quickly rolled the scroll to another passage of scripture and read it to me.

Isaiah 59:2 *But your iniquities have separated between you and your God, and your sins have hid his face from you, that he will not hear.*

He explained to me that the word "iniquities" means "sins," and that sin is simply going against God's will. Sin is listening to the unclean spirit. As long as I allow my sin to remain in my life, God will not hear me. When I see what I am doing is sin, and not just something I want to do, or some habit I have, and get it out of my life, then my relationship with God will begin to get back to where it needs to be.

I want that more than anything, but I am so very afraid of failing again. I have hurt my wife and family once again, and I am not sure they will understand and allow me back into their lives. And how will the people in our Bible study group respond to me if I try to come back? They will think I am someone that cannot be trusted and avoid me. My boss has put up with so much with me that I am not sure my job is even still secure. What if I do make the changes in my life and still end up losing my job and cannot provide for my family?

The fear that gripped me just thinking about all of the problems I had created, and facing all those I had hurt, was overwhelming. It was the same fear that I had when I sat on the shore and watched Jesus sail away, knowing that He told me to go home, but not knowing how I could. The fear of rejection is one of the most powerful things a person can face.

It didn't take long for my friend to point out to me that I was doing, at that very moment, what got me into all of the trouble in the first place. I was listening to the unclean spirit as it placed thoughts into my mind and heart; thoughts that were denying what God's Word plainly showed me was truth. The unclean spirit *never* gives up; it *never* will admit defeat!

My friend then showed me another verse in the scriptures that put everything into perspective as to what needed to be done.

2 Chronicles 7:14 *If my people, which are called by my name, shall humble themselves, and pray, and seek my face, and turn from their wicked ways; then will I hear from heaven, and will forgive their sin, and will heal their land.*

I needed to set my pride aside, and humble myself before God. I needed to admit to God, as well as to myself, that I had sinned; that my actions, thoughts, and attitudes were completely wrong in God's sight. I had been avoiding praying to God in an honest way; seeking His will, but instead was asking Him to bless my will and my actions. I must humble myself and pray; genuinely present myself before God seeking His forgiveness and will. He has promised in that verse that if

I will do that, He will hear and heal the hurt that has been caused.

As I laid on the bed that night, sleep was far from me. All I wanted to do was talk with God, and allow Him to guide my thoughts. I didn't know how things would work out; but I knew they would, because God was in charge. Instead of my priority being my work, I desired to focus on God and His love for me. The feeling of anger that I felt towards my wife for not understanding me turned to a deep sense of shame for having put her through that – again. Just the thought of facing her, and trying to let her know how sorry I was for by behavior, made me ill. I tried role-playing what I could say to her, and what her reactions could be, until I drifted off to sleep.

The next morning, as my friend and I ate breakfast, I noticed that his family was not home. He told me they had gone early that morning to see her parents across town and would not be back until later that afternoon. We had the house all to ourselves, and he didn't have to go to work that day. We took our morning drink and went outside under a tree, and talked most of the day. I had so many questions for him about how I could know for sure I was forgiven by God, as well as how to get back into favor with my wife and kids. I appreciated that none of his answers to my questions were his own opinion, even though that would have been accepted with much value. For every situation I presented to him, he would pull out the scroll, and he seemed to know just the right spot to find exactly what I needed. I may have been able to disagree with his opinion, but how can I honestly disagree with the Word of God?

It was not going to be easy trying to fix all that had been damaged. It was certainly not difficult for God to fix it; but since other human beings, and their feelings and emotions are involved, it may be very difficult with them.

Everything in life carries with it consequences. He showed me Isaiah 1:19-20.

Isaiah 1:19-20 *If ye be willing and obedient, ye shall eat the good of the land: (20) But if ye refuse and rebel, ye shall be devoured with the sword: for the mouth of the LORD hath spoken it.*

The consequence of being obedient to God's Word and leadership in my life is God's blessings. The consequence of disobedience and rebellion is to be devoured "with the sword." He explained to me that God's Word is often referred to as the "sword of the Lord." The consequences of rebelling against God's Word are not only the destruction of your marriage and family relations, your church and social life, but could cause you to die physically.

It became very clear that any change that was to take place depended upon me, and my response to God's leadership in my life. My stubborn pride had kept the selfish thoughts from the unclean spirit alive in my mind. My actions had been based upon a lie, and now the consequences in my life were very apparent. My relationship with my wife and family had suffered extreme damage, as well as the possibility of losing my job. These thoughts weighed heavily on my mind and heart constantly as we talked.

My friend told me that there is only one thing in life that counts, and that one thing is the foundation upon which everything else is built. That one thing is my relationship with God. It isn't just knowing that God exists, because even the devil knows that to be a fact. My relationship with God is never based on my ability to keep His laws and commandments, since God knows that I can't because of sin in my life. My relationship with God can only be based upon one thing, and that is love.

I thought of my relationship with my wife, and considered what it was based upon. It wasn't a relationship built upon me doing chores for her, or upon the fact that I worked hard to earn money, or even that I bought her nice things. My relationship with my wife is based upon the love I have for her, as well as recognizing and cherishing the love she has for me. For a relationship to be based upon love, it must be a mutual love. It cannot be one sided.

God's love for me is so apparent. God saw me in the tombs, totally under the control of the unclean spirit, He loved me so very much that He sent His only Son, Jesus, all the way across the Sea of Galilee, through a terrible storm, just to deliver me from the bondage I was under. God loved me before I ever even knew about Him. How can I not love Him back?

Things began to make sense to me the more my friend and I talked. I could see very clearly that I had simply moved my focus from Jesus to myself. All of the trouble began when I stopped loving to tell what Jesus had done for me that day on the shore. I was still trying to tell others, but it was not with the same passion I had in the beginning. I could see that it was because I had turned my focus onto what the unclean spirit was putting into my head; the thoughts of self, instead of thoughts of God.

All the time I was thinking God was not hearing and answering my prayers, He actually was. I was praying to get out of the situation I was in; that my wife and I would get together again; that my kids would love me again; and that my job would be successful again. Everything only got worse and my relationships became more distant. The unclean spirit was telling me through the thoughts it was putting into my mind, that God doesn't love me, that He doesn't care about me anymore because I have done too much bad for Him to ever care for me again. Actually, just the opposite was happening, and I was too blinded by the thoughts of the unclean spirit to realize it.

I was expecting everything to be worked out all of a sudden; but God wanted to address my problem at the very root, so it would be properly destroyed. If my heart was not dealt with, and if I was not able to realize that the entire problem was me turning away from God, and from my love relationship with Him, the problem would be back, and probably more seriously. I didn't realize that God was at work in my life all of the time, using the circumstances that I had allowed myself to get into for His good.

As I shared my thoughts with my friend, he once again showed me a verse of scripture.

Isaiah 55:8 *For my thoughts are not your thoughts, neither are your ways my ways, saith the LORD.*

My job isn't to try to figure out what God is going to do. My job is to keep my focus upon Him and continually work on my love relationship with Him, and allow Him to work out His plan in my life. Instead of focusing my attention on my relationship with my wife and kids, I need to center my attention on my personal relationship with God. From that foundation, God will build all of the other relationships in my life the way they need to be built for His glory.

As I considered my relationship with my wife and how good it had been, I thought about how it got that way. I loved her very much the day we married, but now, over twenty years later, my love for her is so much greater. How did that happen? It was not easy all of the time, as she will be quick to point out. Our relationship with each other has developed in love because we have spent so much time together. That is the key to any relationship, but especially my relationship with God. Spending time together is not always easy, since the unclean spirit will do all it can to let me know how busy I am, and what all I could get done in the time I set aside to meet with God. But that is the entire point; it is the unclean spirit that draws me away from my relationship with God.

Doing the right thing in my life is a matter of spending time with God. My prayer needs to change from, "Get me out of this situation, restore my marriage, get me back with my kids." to "Lord, what would you have me to do? What are you teaching me today so I can follow you better?" The key to getting my life back on track is to submit myself to God in all things and humbly follow His leadership.

I don't understand why He is allowing these things to happen to me; but I know for certain that He loves me, and that He always is trying to develop me, never to destroy me. As I turn my focus to God in my heart, and as I set my will upon doing His will as He reveals it to me, I can be assured that He will be honored through my life.

Chapter 16   Final Thoughts

As I have shared my story with you, it is my prayer that you will see some of what God is doing in your life within what I have gone through. If I can leave you with one final thought, it would be centered around the word "trust." There are two applications of that word I would like to share with you.

First, you must place your trust in Jesus Christ to have done exactly what He said He did for you. The only thing that will keep you away from a love-based relationship with God is your sin. God cannot look upon sin or anything that is sinful because of His pure holiness. That presented a situation for God since He wants to have a personal relationship with you. God sent His only Son, who came voluntarily, to be born as a human being, live a completely sinless life, shed His sinless blood on the cross, die, be buried, and rise from the dead, all for you! Innocent blood was the price that is demanded by God in His holiness and justice, to pay for your sin. You cannot earn God's forgiveness since you cannot pay the price; your blood is sinful blood. If you try to work your way to obtain God's forgiveness, good deeds outweighing bad ones, you are using the wrong thing to pay for your sin.

For example, let's say that you have a garden and grow some really great tomatoes; the best in all of the county. One day you get your electric bill, so you take a basket of your very best tomatoes to the electric company, put them on the counter with the bill, and ask that the bill be marked "paid." Will they do it? Of course not. Why? You used the wrong currency. They want money, not tomatoes. It is the same with God. The price demanded by God for your sin is innocent blood, not your good works.

Jesus paid the price God demanded with the proper "currency;" therefore, your sin account is paid in full. Have you placed your complete trust in that? It is the only way you will ever have a personal relationship with God here on this earth, as well as the only way you will ever be permitted into God's presence in heaven when you die.

The second application of the word "trust" is what you need to establish with those whom you have offended in your life by your actions. You cannot do harm, physically or emotionally, to another person, and expect them to just set their hurt aside because you have told them you have changed. You must "prove" it to them over a period of time by actually living within the personal, love-based relationship with God that He wants to have with you. How much time will that take? A lifetime! As you continue to focus on your personal relationship with God, He will direct the hearts of others, as well as the circumstances of life to conform to His will for you.

Isaiah 55:8-11 *For my thoughts are not your thoughts, neither are your ways my ways, saith the LORD. (9) For as the heavens are higher than the earth, so are my ways higher than your ways, and my thoughts than your thoughts. (10) For as the rain cometh down, and the snow from heaven, and returneth not thither, but watereth the earth, and maketh it bring forth and bud, that it may give seed to the sower, and bread to the eater: (11) So shall my word be that goeth forth out of my mouth: it shall not return unto me void, but it shall accomplish that which I please, and it shall prosper in the thing whereto I sent it.*

Matthew 6:33 *But seek ye first the kingdom of God, and his righteousness; and all these things shall be added unto you.*

I cannot know exactly how my situation will work out, any more than I know how yours will. However, this one thing I do know: As I keep my focus on Jesus, continue to build my love relationship with Him, and allow Him to lead in my life unconditionally, His will and plan for me will be accomplished. Simply follow Jesus!

-James-

Now Available:

UNMASKING THE UNCLEAN SPIRIT WITHIN YOU
Study Course
By Chaplain Tim Klink

A 13-Lesson Interactive
Study Course – 92 pages –
Spiral Bound

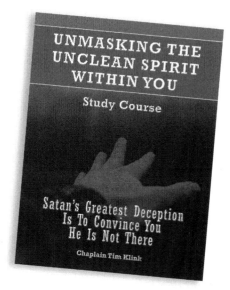

- ➤ Individual Study
- ➤ Small Group Study
- ➤ Teen Studies
- ➤ Adult Sunday School Class
- ➤ Mid-Week Bible Study

UNMASKING THE UNCLEAN SPIRIT WITHIN YOU –
STUDY COURSE considers many of **the most vital areas of your life** and how the unclean spirit subtly does its damaging work *without you being aware of its presence.*
Contents:

Lesson 1   What is the Unclean Spirit?
Lesson 2   The Unclean Spirit in Fear and Doubt
Lesson 3   The Unclean Spirit in Your Thoughts
Lesson 4   The Unclean Spirit in Salvation
Lesson 5   The Unclean Spirit in Anger
Lesson 6   The Unclean Spirit in Power
Lesson 7   The Unclean Spirit in Pleasure/Leisure
Lesson 8   The Unclean Spirit in Money
Lesson 9   The Unclean Spirit in Family
Lesson 10 The Unclean Spirit in Friends
Lesson 11 The Unclean Spirit in Marriage
Lesson 12 The Unclean Spirit in Work
Lesson 13 The Unclean Spirit in Worship

For more information contact Chaplain Tim Klink,
Prison Discipleship Ministry, P.O. Box 645, Massillon OH 44648

Email: timklink@fellowshipbaptistchurch.org